Read On . . . History

Recent Titles in Libraries Unlimited Read On Series
Barry Trott, Series Editor

Read On . . . Historical Fiction: Reading Lists for Every Taste
Brad Hooper

Read On . . . Horror Fiction: Reading Lists for Every Taste
June Michele Pulliam and Anthony J. Fonseca

Read On . . . Fantasy Fiction: Reading Lists for Every Taste
Neil Hollands

Read On . . . Crime Fiction: Reading Lists for Every Taste
Barry Trott

Read On . . . Women's Fiction: Reading Lists for Every Taste
Rebecca Vnuk

Read On . . . Life Stories: Reading Lists for Every Taste
Rosalind Reisner

Read On . . . Science Fiction: Reading Lists for Every Taste
Steven A. Torres-Roman

Read On . . . Audiobooks: Reading Lists for Every Taste
Joyce G. Saricks

Read On . . . Graphic Novels: Reading Lists for Every Taste
Abby Alpert

Read On . . . Biography: Reading Lists for Every Taste
Rick Roche

Read On . . . Speculative Fiction for Teens: Reading Lists for Every Taste
Jamie Kallio

Read On . . . History

Reading Lists for Every Taste

Tina Frolund

Read On Series
Barry Trott, Series Editor

 LIBRARIES UNLIMITED

AN IMPRINT OF ABC-CLIO, LLC
Santa Barbara, California • Denver, Colorado • Oxford, England

Library of Congress Cataloging-in-Publication Data

Frolund, Tina.
  Read on . . . history : reading lists for every taste / Tina Frolund.
    pages cm. — (Read on series)
  Includes index.
  ISBN 978-1-61069-034-8 (pbk.) — ISBN 978-1-61069-432-2 (ebook)
1. History—Bibliography.   2. United States—History—Bibliography.
3. Readers' advisory services—United States.   4. Public libraries—
United States—Book lists.   I. Title.
  Z6201.F77   2013
  [D21]
  016.9—dc23   2013029492

ISBN: 978-1-61069-034-8
EISBN: 978-1-61069-432-2

17 16 15 14   2 3 4 5

This book is also available on the World Wide Web as an eBook.
Visit www.abc-clio.com for details.

Libraries Unlimited
An Imprint of ABC-CLIO, LLC

ABC-CLIO, LLC
130 Cremona Drive, P.O. Box 1911
Santa Barbara, California 93116-1911

This book is printed on acid-free paper (∞)

Manufactured in the United States of America

Contents

Series Foreword

Welcome to Libraries Unlimited's Read On series of fiction and nonfiction genre guides for readers' advisors and for readers. The Read On series introduces readers and those who work with them to new ways of looking at books, genres, and reading interests.

Over the past decade, readers' advisory services have become vital in public libraries. A quick glance at the schedule of any library conference at the state or national level will reveal a wealth of programs on various aspects of connecting readers to books they will enjoy. Working with unfamiliar genres or types of reading can be a challenge, particularly for those new to the field. Equally, readers may find it a bit overwhelming to look for books outside their favorite authors and preferred reading interests. The titles in the Read On series offer you a new way to approach reading:

- they introduce you a broad sampling of materials available in a given genre;
- they offer you new directions to explore in a genre—through appeal features and unconventional topics;
- they help readers' advisors better understand and navigate genres with which they are less familiar; and
- they provide reading lists that you can use to create quick displays, include on your library websites and in the library newsletter, or to hand out to readers.

The lists in the Read On series are arranged in sections based on appeal characteristics—story, character, setting, and language (as described in Joyce Saricks's *Reader's Advisory Services in the Public Library*, 3rd ed., ALA Editions, 2005), with a fifth section on mood/tone. These are hidden elements of a book that attract readers. Remember that a book can have multiple appeal factors; and sometimes readers are drawn to a particular book for several factors, while other times for only one. In the Read On lists, titles are placed according to their primary appeal characteristics, and then put into a list that reflects common reading interests. So if you are working with a reader who loves fantasy that features quests for magical objects or a reader who is interested in memoirs with a strong sense of place, you will be able to find a list of titles whose main appeal centers around this search. Each list indicates a title that is an especially good starting place for readers, an exemplar of that appeal characteristic.

Story is perhaps the most basic appeal characteristic. It relates to the plot of the book—What are the elements of the tale? Is the emphasis more on the people or the situations? Is the story action focused or more interior? Is it funny? Scary?

Many readers are drawn to the books they love by the characters. The character appeal reflects such aspects as whether there are lots of characters or only a single main character; are the characters easily recognizable types? Do the characters grow and change over the course of the story? What are the characters' occupations?

Setting covers a range of elements that might appeal to readers. What is the time period or geographic locale of the tale? How much does the author describe the surroundings of the story? Does the reader feel as though he or she is "there" when reading the book? Are there special features such as the monastic location of Ellis Peters's Brother Cadfael Mysteries series or the small-town setting of Jan Karon's Mitford series?

Although not traditionally considered an appeal characteristic, mood is important to readers as well. It relates to how the author uses the tools of narrative—language, pacing, story, and character—to create a feeling for the work. Mood can be difficult to quantify because the reader brings his or her own feelings to the story as well. Mood really asks, how does the book make the reader feel? Creepy? Refreshed? Joyful? Sad?

Finally, the language appeal brings together titles where the author's writing style draws the reader. This can be anything from a lyrical prose style with lots of flourishes to a spare use of language à la Hemingway. Humor, snappy dialog, word-play, recipes, and other language elements all have the potential to attract readers.

Dig into these lists. Use them to find new titles and authors in a genre that you love, or as a guide to expand your knowledge of a new type of writing. Above all, read, enjoy, and remember—never apologize for your reading tastes!

—*Barry Trott*
Series Editor

Introduction

History: The branch of knowledge dealing with past events.
—From Dictionary.com

The past is full of facts, dates, causes, and effects that can be effectively presented as data; textbooks and reference books excel at this. But books written about the past do not have to read like textbooks. In fact, there are many reading choices now for readers who love history but don't love boring books. Motivated readers could always reach back to seek out the gracious prose and opinionated insights of Edward Gibbon, the crystalline clarity of Barbara Tuchman, and the informed compassion of C. V. Wedgewood—examples of authors from earlier eras who created books of great appeal while maintaining strict standards of scholarship. Today's historians, scholars, journalists, authors, and editors also strive to present the past using dynamic prose and exciting structure. David McCullough, Robert Caro, Alison Weir, and Mark Kurlansky are just a few of the authors writing history today who write to enthrall a reader and appeal to a wide readership. They are not only devoted to accurate historical explorations, but also committed to sharing their information in the most enthralling way they can. They and many other writers excel at choosing the most compelling episodes from history and presenting them with vitality and insight, crafting history into great reads. This book offers you access to the universe of great historical reads.

The Growth of Narrative History

Narrative history, history that emphasizes story over recitations of facts, is not new, but attention to the genre has grown and continues to expand. Simon Winchester's *The Madman and the Professor* (1998), Laura Hillenbrand's *Seabiscuit: An American Legend* (2001), and Erik Larson's *Devil in the White City* (2004), all became best sellers—a difficult status for a history book to achieve. Readers, reviewers, booksellers, librarians, editors, publishers, and other writers, all took notice. The demand for intriguing, high-interest books about the past took off and production has, delightfully, increased.

In this book, you will find descriptions of more than 400 titles written with the reader in mind. Some of the books are written by bona fide historians, some by journalists, some of the books have a more scholarly tone, and some are truly aimed at a popular readership. All are written by skilled writers trying their best to shape their material to interest readers.

Criteria for Selection

Books were chosen for inclusion in this book with the following criteria in mind:

- Readability—All of the books contain writing of very high quality and high interest. Every book is engaging and also enlightening.
- Subject appeal to general readers not specialists.
- Accurate information from well-documented and verifiable sources. Readers of history don't mind, in fact prefer and have even been known to enjoy bibliographies, authors' notes on sources, even footnotes.
- Recent publication date and current availability. The majority of books in this book are in print and were published after 2000. Classic works of history that have been reprinted are included, proving they are interesting, enduring books that retain the power to captivate contemporary readers. And though one or two of the titles are out-of-print, they are commonly available from libraries and can be found in used bookstores.
- Historical fiction is included. Though the titles in each list are predominantly nonfiction, fiction titles are included in many of the lists. Skilled authors of historical fiction can take facts and weave a story that immerses the reader into the past or the life of a character from history.
- Good Reviews—Each of these books received positive reviews in a major newspaper such as *The New York Times*, *The Washington Post*, or *The Wall Street Journal*; a history journal like *American History* or *History Today*; or a major reviewing source like *Booklist*, *Publishers Weekly*, *Library Journal*, or *Kirkus*.

How to Use This Book

Appeal Factors

The raw material of the past can be read as love stories, family sagas, mysteries, crimes, gentle stories, and even animal stories. This book helps you find the kinds of books you like to read by using the five appeal factors—character, story, setting, language, and tone or mood—recognized by librarians and readers as an effective way to match books to readers. Appeal characteristics go to the heart of why a reader is drawn to a certain book. Do you like to read stories about people? Turn to the lists in Chapter Two. Do you prefer a short book? Check out the books listed in "Long Ago for Short Attention Spans—History Under 300 Pages" (Chapter Four). Maybe you like the challenge of a unique narrative structure? Read the books listed in "Unusual Tellings" (Chapter Four). Are you a student of the role of women in history? Turn to the books listed in "Well-Behaved Women Seldom Make History" (Chapter Two) to read about rabble-rouser Mother Jones and America's first teenager Alice Roosevelt Long-worth or consult "It's Not Easy Being Queen" (Chapter Two) to get the inside story on Cleopatra, the rebellious Christina of Sweden, and the gracious last queen of Hawaii.

Lists

This is a book of lists. Readers, and those who serve them, should see each list as a beginning place, not a comprehensive or complete catalog. Each list invites further exploration. Every list could have been twice as long. Each list could also have reached back farther into publishing time. All of the lists are open-ended as newer books are being published every day by brilliant writers and bold publishers uncovering new stories from the past, telling old stories in new ways, and exploring the boundary where fact and narrative happily meet.

As an example of how the lists can help you consider "On the Briny—Stories Set at Sea" (Chapter Three). There you will find *Six Frigates* by Ian Toll a rip-roaring, saltwater soaked story that is a nonfiction historical account of the founding of the U.S. Navy. Also listed are *We, the Drowned*, a contemporary novel, by Jensen Carsten about men and women who lived off the sea and *The Hard Way Around: The Passages of Joshua Slocum* by Geoffrey Wolff, the biography of a famous seaman. In traditional bibliographic thinking, these books might not be grouped together, one is fiction the others nonfiction, one is American history, one is a Danish novel, one is biography. But if we consider the appeal of the books, each book set at sea in the world of men, ships, and the oceans, the books are perfectly matched and readers who enjoy one of these titles will likely enjoy the others and be thankful for the introduction to them.

Index

To enhance access, a master index of authors, titles, and series titles is included. Use the index to find a favorite author, a familiar title, or a series. Check the index to find lists of related books that share the appeal characteristics and other qualities you want to explore.

Who Will Use This Book?

- Readers who already enjoy reading history and readers who are new to the genre and want to begin an exploration will find this book to be a valuable resource.
- Librarians charged with reader's advisory duties can use this book to expand their knowledge of current history authors and titles, and to recommend books to a wide range of readers—casual readers, history buffs, young adults, and students. Librarians can also use the lists for collection development decisions about selection and retention and for help creating lists of recommended reading or displays to market the nonfiction collection.
- Young adults can use this book to find high-interest reading for school assignments and for pleasure reading. Books with particular appeal to readers in their late teens are indicated as Y A.
- Book groups can use this book in many different ways. The group may want to work through an entire list selecting a different title each month. Or the group may want to assign each book in a list to a different member creating a discussion of the overall appeal or theme and giving members of the group exposure to multiple titles. Groups who usually select books that emphasize Character or Story may want to challenge themselves by choosing something from the Setting or Language chapters.

Symbols Used

▶ A book that exemplifies the characteristics of its list.

🏆 A book that has been acknowledged with a major literary award. Awards include the Pulitzer Prize, National Book Award, Pritzker Military Library Literature Award, Sidewise Award for Alternate History, and the Caldecott Medal.

Y A A book that will be interesting and appropriate for older teen readers.

📚 A book that is sure to create discussion and interaction in your book group.

Chapter One

Story

Do you remember reading history and slipping into a catatonic state brought on by the unceasing parade of obscure places, dull facts, and dead people that made up the contents of your history book? Well, those days are over.

In recent years, history has stepped away from the occasionally dreary world of academe and stepped in to the spotlight of popular reading. History books now incorporate narrative techniques that compel readers to keep reading—a story with a beginning, middle, and end; character depictions that make you want to know more; and intercutting of events to create interest and tension—in other words, good storytelling not just fact after fact after fact. What, after all, is history but a story, the story of human events?

At the same time, the books have retained the scholarly apparatus that gives them the stature of substantial nonfiction. Notes, bibliographies, a trained historian or learned seeker's explanation of cause and effect, and placement of an issue or event into context, all these things will always matter for historical explorations; but now it can all come in the package of entertaining reading as well. The best history writing of the past always had this combination of scholarship and entertainment, but today more and more writers, journalists, historians, editors, and publishers strive to capture readers through terrific storytelling. History has never been more enjoyable to read. From the personal, the national, the global, to the cosmic, the books in this section tell great stories without sacrificing credibility, scholarship, or authority.

Unsolved History—Mysteries in History

Historians have sought answers to these mysteries for—in some instances—centuries and with each passing year updated scientific techniques, and newly discovered documents and evidence expose a little more of the truth. Readers who love mysteries and suspense will love these nonfiction stories of unsolved history.

Cadbury, Deborah.
▶ *The Lost King of France: How DNA Solved the Mystery of the Murdered Son of Louis XVI and Marie Antoinette.* 2002. St. Martin's. 978-0312283124. 288pp.

This is the story of the heart-wrenching death of a little boy and the modern day efforts to confirm his identity. The little boy was the son of Marie Antoinette, destined to be King Louis XVII of France, but instead imprisoned and forced to endure starvation and abuse at the hands of the representatives of the new republic until his death at the age of 10. The mystery? Was it really the Dauphin who died in the prison cell or had the real prince escaped his captors? For decades following the death, imposters stepped forward to claim the birthright of this prince of France. It takes modern DNA science to find an answer. Cadbury offers a well-researched, well-documented, and compellingly told story of the fate of little Louis-Charles.

Cookman, Scott.
Ice Blink: The Tragic Fate of Sir John Franklin's Lost Polar Expedition. 2000. Wiley and Son. 0471377902. 244pp.

Franklin and 128 men sailed in 1845 seeking the elusive Northwest Passage. Their course would take them from Greenland to Baffin Bay and into the frigid Arctic waters where all would perish. Why? Their ships were the most modern and they were well provisioned for the journey; the crews were experienced; and Franklin, veteran of three previous Arctic voyages, seemed the perfect leader for this endeavor. Yet, every man died. Cookman tells the gripping tale of what may have happened on this polar expedition gone terribly wrong, a mystery that has haunted the history of exploration for almost 175 years.

Hicks, Brian.
Ghost Ship: The Mysterious True Story of the Mary Celeste and Her Missing Crew. 2004. Ballantine (paperback). 978-0345466655. 304pp.

In December 1872, the *Mary Celeste* left Staten Island bound for Genoa, Italy, with 1,700 barrels of commercial alcohol. Before she reached her destination something happened—but no one knows what. The *Mary Celeste* was intercepted foundering in the ocean swells 600 miles off the coast of Portugal, abandoned, and no souls on board. The captain, his crew of seven experienced sailors, and two passengers—the captain's wife and two-year-old daughter—had all disappeared. The cargo and their personal belongings were untouched.

Hicks tells the suspenseful story and offers his theory of what happened to the *Mary Celeste*, a maritime mystery that has baffled generations of sailors and landlubbers.

Horn, James P. P.
A Kingdom Strange: The Brief and Tragic History of the Lost Colony of Roanoke. 2010. Basic Books. 978-0465004850. 304pp.

Roanoke Island off the coast of modern day North Carolina was the site of the first English settlement in North America. Backed by Sir Walter Raleigh, the colony existed for less than three years; by 1590, the colony had disappeared. Did the 115 settlers peacefully integrate into local Native American tribes? Were they killed by the Spanish? Did they perish at sea attempting to return to England in one of their small ships intended only for exploring the coast? Did they die from hunger or disease? If so, who dismantled the houses and fortifications? A lasting American mystery.

King, Greg and Penny Wilson.
The Resurrection of the Romanovs: Anastasia, Anna Anderson, and the World's Greatest Royal Mystery. 2011. Wiley. 978-0470444986. 397pp.

The story of Anna Anderson claimed the attention of the world for many years. Was Anna Anderson really Grand Duchess Anastasia, youngest daughter of the Tsar of Russia, and survivor of the brutal murder that took her family, or was she a Polish factory worker of unstable mental health but enough physical similarity to the lost princess to pass as her? King and Wilson tell the story of the massacred royal family and the claims of Anna Anderson and her supporters in this fascinating analysis of one of history's most lasting imposter stories. For more about the final days of the Russian royals, read *The Romanovs: The Final Chapter* (1995) by Robert K. Massie.

Weir, Alison.
The Princes in the Tower. 1992. Ballantine (paperback). 978-0345391780. 287pp.

One of history's enduring questions is what happened to the princes in the Tower? In 1483, 12-year-old Edward—King Edward V of England whose reign lasted less than 3 months—and his 9-year-old brother Richard were living in the Tower of London awaiting Edward's coronation. After a few months residence, they disappeared, never to be seen again. Weir—one of Britain's best popular historians—sifts through all the evidence, addresses every suspect and theory, and offers her well-reasoned conclusion in this mystery set during the War of the Roses that reads like a legal thriller.

Art and Bones—Objects with a Past

The past is filled with art and bones. How these objects are lost and found, preserved, and coveted make great stories of gentle adventure.

Charney, Noah.
Stealing the Mystic Lamb: The True Story of the World's Most Coveted Masterpiece. 2010. Public Affairs Books. 978-1586488000. 318pp.

War and art are history's eternal opponents. Beautiful things created during peace are looted during war. *The Ghent Altarpiece*, painted by Jan Van Eyck in the 1430s, is a room-sized work of oil paintings on wooden panels, a complex mix of symbolism and realism depicting among other scenes the Annunciation, the adoration of the Mystic Lamb, and an angelic choir. It has endured being damaged, broken apart, pawned, stolen, hidden, and recovered multiple times. Charney details the traumatic and triumphant 500-year history of this monumental piece of art.

Chevalier, Tracy.
Remarkable Creatures. 2010. Dutton. 0525951458. 320pp. FICTION ⬨

Two women of different classes, experiences, and education find a friendship in their shared love and skill at hunting fossils. The cliffs of early 19th-century Lyme Regis, England, were the setting where Mary Anning a self-educated, working girl found the remains of a large reptile and Elizabeth Philpott, better educated and more socially prominent, became Anning's champion. Chevalier shows the chauvinism of men against women and religion against doubters in this fictional account of Mary Anning's life and discoveries. Chevalier is a noted author of historical fiction who often places art and artists at the center of her stories.

Clark, Catherine Scott and Adrian Levy.
The Amber Room: The Fate of the World's Greatest Treasure. 2004. Walker and Co. 978-0802714244. 416pp.

The mystery of what happened to the Amber Room is part art history, part adventure story. The dazzling panels of carved amber, the golden resin from ancient trees, resided in Catherine the Great's palace in St. Petersburg. In 1941, as Nazi's approached and other irreplaceable palace treasures were being frantically evacuated, the Amber Room, its panels too brittle to be moved, was covered over and left behind. Quickly discovered by the invading troops, the room was dismantled and sent to Germany—or was it? Investigative journalists Clark and Levy trudge through snowy post–Soviet Russia talking to aging curators and party men and reading through archives of newly declassified documents to piece together the true fate of the magnificent Amber Room.

Edsel, Robert M. and Bret Witter.
The Monuments Men: Allied Heroes, Nazi Thieves and the Greatest Treasure Hunt in History. 2009. Center Street. 978-1599951492. 496pp.

Nazi's loved art. Estimates place the number of moveable art and cultural objects that the Nazis looted at 5 million! The Nazi plan was to keep what they considered "finest" and destroy what they deemed "degenerate." It became the task of the men and women of the Allied force called the MFAA (Monuments,

Fine Art and Archives) to protect, track down, and recover this booty. Members of this force were artists, curators, educators, archivists, and scholars who volunteered to serve. Edsel tells the exciting story of this largely successful mission to save the cultural heritage of mankind.

Fowler, Brenda.
Iceman: Uncovering the Life and Times of a Prehistoric Man Found in an Alpine Glacier. 2000. University of Chicago Press (paperback). 978-0226258232. 330pp.

An archaeological discovery becomes a forensic thriller as modern science meets prehistory in this story about the well-preserved remains of a man found by hikers in Austria in 1991. Named Ötzi by the press, what he ate, what he wore, what he carried with him as he traversed the mountain pass, why he was there, where he was going, and how he died were all questions scientists and scholars hoped to answer as they studied this amazingly well-preserved but poorly excavated find. Fowler writes about the possible life Ötzi led 5,000 years ago, about the academics and scientists who quarreled about the best way to study him, and about the politicians who bickered about his true, and potential future tourist-site, home.

Myerson, Daniel.
In the Valley of the Kings: Howard Carter and the Mystery of King Tutankhamun's Tomb. 2009. Ballantine Books. 978-0345476937. 230pp.

In 1922, after seven years of searching, Howard Carter, working for his patron Lord Carnarvon, found the greatest Egyptian tomb yet discovered. The unearthing of this royal tomb and its marvelous treasures captured the imagination of the world. This is the story of the personalities and petty politics that played out during and after the discovery and of the irascible and, to many of his contemporaries, unpleasant personality of Howard Carter and the impact his historic discovery had upon his life and the world.

O'Connor, Anne-Marie.
The Lady in Gold: The Extraordinary Tale of Gustav Klimt's Masterpiece, Portrait of Adele Bloch-Bauer. 2012. Knopf. 978-0307265647. 368pp.

Gustav Klimt was the bad boy of Viennese society and his paintings were sought after by all; to have a portrait done by Klimt was an extraordinary honor. In 1907, Klimt painted the portrait of wealthy society woman Adele Bloch-Bauer, her face and form surrounded by the shimmering gold and silver that makes the painting so extraordinary. Enter World War II and the Nazis. O'Connor tells the absorbing tale of the painting, the society that created it, the Nazi looting, and the legal battle to restore the work to its owners.

Pringle, Heather.
▶ *The Mummy Congress: Science, Obsession, and the Everlasting Dead.* 2001. Hyperion. 0786865512. 368pp.

Journalist Pringle attends the Mummy Congress—a meeting of mummy experts, scientists, scholars, and enthusiasts—to acquaint herself with the world of the preserved dead. She learns about the Chinchorro mummies found in Chile and Peru, many of them children, who are the oldest discovered mummified human remains; that Chairman Mao's embalming was not a success; and that the bodies of many saints deemed "incorruptible" have actually never decayed. A seemingly gruesome topic is given a fascinating and respectful presentation by Pringle, a graceful writer with a talent for capturing an interesting story. It includes many photographs.

Earth, Wind, and Fire—Natural Disasters

We inhabit a planet that occasionally hiccups. When it does, the lives and trappings of humanity are little impediment to the resettling of the earth. These stories depict the courage and the tragedy inherent when societies endure a natural disaster.

Brown, Curt.
So Terrible a Storm: A Tale of Fury on Lake Superior. 2008. Voyageur Press. 978-0760332436. 320pp.

Over Thanksgiving weekend in 1905, Lake Superior was ravaged by a storm with savagely high winds, unrelenting waves, and freezing snow and rain. Almost 30 ships were still on the lake hauling ore or coal to ports like Duluth and Sault Sainte Marie, making final runs before the real winter weather ended the shipping season. Brown tells the harrowing tales of several ships that rode through the massive gale, some surviving and some not. Brown makes a point of exploring the unique world of the Great Lakes, their history, geography, and spirit in this fascinating but upsetting tale.

Krist, Gary.
The White Cascade: The Great Northern Railway Disaster and America's Deadliest Avalanche. 2007. Henry Holt and Co. 978-0805077056. 336pp. [Y][A]

Avalanches can descend mountains unobserved and unremarked. In 1910, two trains traveling west from Spokane to Seattle were trapped by weather in the little Cascade Mountain train depot town of Wellington, Washington. For days, the passengers and Great Northern Railway employees lived on the snowbound trains, evaluating their options—could they hike out or should they wait for help? But nature ended the debate when an avalanche slammed down the mountain at night and killed men, women, and children in a crush of snow, ice, felled trees, and crumpled train cars. Krist tells a tale of pathos and drama from an era with no radios, no helicopters, and few safety regulations or equipment, when the decision to wait it out led to the United States' deadliest avalanche.

Laskin, David.
The Children's Blizzard. 2004. Harper Collins. 0060520752. 307pp. ⓎⒶ
    Weather happens because the earth's atmosphere continually seeks equilibrium, contrasting temperatures and air pressures always try to balance one another. On January 12, 1888, on the Dakota and Nebraska prairie, arctic cold air from Canada and tropically warm air from Mexico converged with a low pressure over the plains and the quest for equilibrium caused the temperature to fall 18 degrees in 3 minutes. The result was human tragedy. Children who had walked to school without hats and coats because the weather was unseasonably warm that morning died trying to get home that afternoon; grown-ups perished yards from shelter, unable to see a path through the snow; cattle froze where they stood, dying by the hundreds. Laskin passionately narrates the science of the weather story and the emotion of the human story.

Palmer, James.
Heaven Cracks, Earth Shakes: The Tangshan Earthquake and the Death of Mao's China. 2012. Basic Books. 978-0465014781. 273pp.
    "The 23 seconds of the earthquake were probably the most concentrated instant of destruction humanity has ever known." A quarter of a million people killed, buildings flattened, a city needing to be rebuilt, but more importantly to Chinese thinking, an omen of upcoming dynastic political change. Palmer's book is as much about the end of Mao's reign in China as about the earthquake in Tangshan in 1976. A gripping account of a natural disaster that ranks as the earthquake with the largest death toll in the 20th century and the final stroke ending the years of Mao's power.

Shrady, Nicholas.
The Last Day: Wrath, Ruin, and Reason in the Great Lisbon Earthquake of 1755. 2008. Viking. 978-0670018512. 228pp.
    On November 1, 1755, around 9:30 on the morning of All Saint's Day when the Catholic inhabitants of Lisbon were crowded into churches, an earthquake struck the city. The quake was rapidly followed by a tsunami that swamped the port city and then by widespread fires. Death estimates are inexact, but the Lisbon earthquake was probably the deadliest in history. More than material destruction, the earthquake caused people of the time to rethink their place in the world—why would God destroy this righteous city? Shrady's small book is an excellent introduction to the mindset and events of the times and to a historically significant natural disaster that motivated one of the first international relief responses—money, material, and aid came in from all over the world—and allowed the city of Lisbon to be rebuilt along purely Enlightenment ideals.

Winchester, Simon.
  ▶ *Krakatoa: The Day the World Exploded, August 27, 1883.* 2003. Harper. 978-0066212852. 432pp.

Considered the largest explosion recorded in human history, the volcanic eruption of Krakatoa in 1883 destroyed islands, sent oceanic waves across the globe, and disrupted weather patterns for years, making winters colder and sunsets more dramatic. Winchester details the environment, the local civilization, and the Dutch colonial culture of Indonesia in the period leading up to the eruption and the aftermath. Winchester is a brilliant, entertainingly digressive nonfiction writer, geologist, and journalist. His subjects are diverse. He has also written about the 1906 San Francisco earthquake, the Yellow River in China, the Atlantic Ocean, and the making of the *Oxford English Dictionary*.

More Precious than Gold

These stores show how men have always sought beauty and wealth. Ignorance, distance, and danger have been little impediment to the discovery or creation of coveted things that proved to be more precious than gold.

Garfield, Simon.
Mauve: How One Man Invented a Color that Changed the World. 2002. Norton (paperback). 978-0393323139. 240pp.

"What use is a color?" In 1856, chemist William Perkin while attempting to find artificial quinine found instead the first man-made dye, a dye derived from coal tar that created a light purple color dubbed mauve. It became a sensation. This accidental discovery made Perkin a wealthy man and created a new industry—chemical research for commercial uses—that would eventually fuel developments in the fields of medicine, photography, explosives, and plastics. Garfield is a cheeky writer and this story of a surprise discovery that created fortunes is agreeable and enlightening.

Gleeson, Janet.
The Arcanum: The Extraordinary True Story. 1999. Warner Books. 0446524999. 324pp.

Johann Frederick Böttger boasted he knew the alchemical formula for creating gold. Augustus II King of Poland and Elector of Saxony wanted that knowledge. He imprisoned Böttger and forced him to experiment for years in the hopes of creating gold. Böttger failed to create gold; but around 1709, he perfected the formula, the Arcanum, for porcelain and the fabulous German production factories of Dresden and Meissen were begun. Porcelain—fine and fragile, translucent and elegant—was rare in 18th-century Europe, and Gleeson crafts an amazing story about a time when a china teacup was worth its weight in gold and a man's freedom.

Greenfield, Amy Butler.
▶ *A Perfect Red: Empire, Espionage and the Quest for the Color of Desire.* 2005. Harper. 978-0060522759. 352pp.

Before mauve was created in a laboratory, man relied on natural dyes to add color and distinction to life. Cochineal, the Mexican scale insect that lives on a cactus and is smaller than a ladybug, offered the perfect red—a color once reserved for cardinals, kings, and society's elite. Greenfield tells how the color was produced by indigenous people, introduced to Europe by Conquistadors, and then refined, coveted, stolen, protected, and fought over in this sweeping story that touches on international history, war, politics, science, and fashion.

Hager, Thomas.
The Alchemy of Air: A Jewish Genius, a Doomed Tycoon, and the Scientific Discovery that Fed the World but Fueled the Rise of Hitler. 2008. Crown. 978-0307351784. 336pp.

Can the Third Reich, global warming, and today's obesity epidemic be blamed on two men who had the noble goal of feeding the world? This engrossing story covers many topics: alchemy, farming, weaponry, the South American guano boom, Nazis, industrial chemistry, two World Wars, and the personal stories of two men—Carl Bosch and Fritz Haber—who discovered the process to create nitrogen fertilizers and unleashed upon the world yet another double-edged sword.

Kurin, Richard.
Hope Diamond: The Legendary History of a Cursed Gem. 2010. Harper Perennial. 0060873523. 400pp.

A crystal taken from deep under the ground where it rested for thousands of years becomes an object of desire when polished, cut, set among other gems, and given a compelling story that includes mystery, intrigue, royalty, danger, glamour, and wealth. The Hope Diamond, now securely housed at the Smithsonian's Natural History Museum where it is visited by thousands of people a day, is one of those coveted and storied gems. Kurin offers the incredible tale of the life of this fabulous gem.

Perman, Stacy.
A Grand Complication: The Race to Build the World's Most Legendary Watch. 2013. Atria. 978-1439190081. 343pp.

Though today we tell time from our cell phones, for several hundred years, watchmakers who could craft the tiny mechanisms needed for a first-class watch were prized and their chronometric creations were the privilege of only the very wealthy. In a sweeping story that encompasses social history, larger-than-life personalities, the exploits of the early 20th century's super rich, and the intricacies of watchmaking and watch collecting, Perman tells the tale of the watch that eventually sold for $11 million—the Graves Supercomplication designed by Patek Philippe and once the most intricate mechanical watch ever created.

Turner, Jack.
Spice: A History of a Temptation. 2004. Harper Collins. 978-0002570671. 448pp.

Pepper, cinnamon, nutmeg, and clove are so common now, but were once the rarest and most coveted of treasures. Turner offers up the grand story of humanity's taste for exotic flavors in his explorations of the historical global quest for spices that once sent men sailing into the unknown with brazen hopes of securing a fortune.

Heroism off the Battlefield—Human Stories from World War II

Everyone is interested in World War II, but not all readers want military history. The intense personal stories in the recent best sellers *Sarah's Key*, *The Guernsey Literary and Potato Peel Society*, and *The Invisible Bridge* attest to the popularity of war stories that are not about the battles. These books offer noncombatant stories of World War II.

Ackerman, Diane.

▶ *The Zookeeper's Wife: A War Story.* 2007. Norton. 978-0393061727. 368pp.

In 1939, when Hitler's army invaded Poland, the Warsaw Zoo was governed by the zookeeper Jan Zabinski and his wife, Antonina. As the war progressed and life in Warsaw became dangerous for everyone and deadly to Jews, the zoo became a refuge; 300 Jews were saved by living in or escaping through the zoo. Written in Ackerman's signature lyrical prose with passages of lush, sensuous description and pulling heavily from memoirs of the protagonists, this is a Holocaust story about human dignity, courage, and kindness in a most unusual setting.

Albright, Madeleine.

Prague Winter: A Personal Story of Remembrance and War, 1937–1948. 2012. Harper. 978-0062030313. 480pp.

The Czechoslovakian girl who grew up to be the U.S. Secretary of State, Madeleine Albright was raised as a Catholic in London during World War II after her parents fled their native country. Albright didn't learn until she was 59 that her family had originally been Jewish and many of her close relatives died in the Nazi death camps. Albright takes us on her journey in this reflective family story that is also a history of Czechoslovakia and World War II told with the large worldview of someone who understands both the geopolitical and personal realities of war.

Cohen, David.

The Escape of Sigmund Freud: Freud's Final Years in Vienna and His Flight from the Nazi Rise. 2012. Overlook Press. 978-1590206737. 272pp.

To confirm he had been treated properly by the Nazi's before leaving Vienna in 1939, Freud wrote, "I most warmly recommend the Gestapo to everybody"—daring irony from a world famous, 82-year-old Jew who was just inches away from escaping with his family to London. Freud's work, his complicated (one could say Freudian) family life, the family's abrupt relocation near the end of his life, and the rise of Nazism in the Viennese milieu are all narrated in riveting prose by Cohen.

Kerr, Philip.
March Violets. 2004 (originally published in 1989). Penguin (paperback). 978-0142004142. 256pp. FICTION
Bernhard Gunther is an ex-cop turned private dick in 1936 Berlin where Nazis are rising, Jews are disappearing, and Bernie in true Raymond Chandler–fashion solves crimes and comments on it all with the jaundiced eye of a noir hero. Gunther goes on to be in seven more hard-boiled Kerr novels. For more thrillers about Europe in the buildup to World War II, consider authors Jonathan Rabb, Alan Furst, and Rebecca Cantrell.

Nagorski, Andrew.
Hitlerland: American Eyewitnesses to the Nazi Rise to Power. 2012. Simon and Schuster. 978-1439191002. 400pp.
Had you been a diplomat, a journalist, or a businessman in Germany in the 1920s or 1930s, would you have comprehended the growing threat? Could you have interpreted the signs of oppression and destruction to come? Many Americans traveled, worked, and resided in Germany between the two World Wars, and Nagorski examines them and their recollections to chart America's awakening to the evolution of Hitler's Germany. An enthralling look at bright people—like Thomas Wolfe, Sinclair Lewis, William Shirer, Howard K Smith, and Charles Lindbergh—in a bad time. For another exploration of this story, read Erik Larson's *In the Garden of the Beasts* (2011).

Weintraub, Stanley.
Pearl Harbor Christmas: A World at War, December 1941. 2011. Da Capo Press. 978-0306820618. 224pp.
With the bombing of Pearl Harbor just days in the past, America finally commits to war. A jubilant Churchill travels by warship through the U-boat–ridden, storm-tossed Atlantic to spend Christmas at the White House and begin the great preparations for world war with America as a full participant. Weintraub offers a snapshot of the days around Christmas in 1941 as Churchill, Roosevelt, and their attendants socialize and plan; diplomats around the world negotiate; Hitler rails at his own generals and troops; and America celebrates one last Christmas before rationing and blackout curtains. Weintraub has created an entire genre of easy-reading narrative history books about wartime Christmases. Read *Silent Night: The Story of the World War I Christmas Truce* (2001) and *George Washington's Christmas Farewell: A Mount Vernon Homecoming, 1783* (2003). Lynne Olson takes a broader look at this episode in the excellent *Citizens of London: The Americans Who Stood with Britain in Its Darkest, Finest Hour* (2011).

Zuckoff, Mitchell.
Lost in Shangri-La: A True Story of Survival, Adventure and the Most Incredible Rescue Mission of World War II. 2011. Harper. 978-0061988349. 400pp.
    Taking a break from the war, several soldiers and WACs based in New Guinea take a sightseeing trip over an enchanting and remote valley, inhabited by primitive tribesman and probably Japanese warriors. But the sightseeing tour devolves into a battle for survival and a test of determination and resolve when the plane goes down. This is a gripping action adventure story that happened parallel to the main action of the war. For another astonishing survival adventure, read Laura Hillenbrand's *Unbroken: A WWII Story of Survival* (2010).

Warriors and Weapons

Since first picking up and throwing a rock, man has sought more efficient ways to fight and kill enemies. These books look at warriors, their weapons, and the tactics of war through history.

Cohen, Richard.
By the Sword: A History of Gladiators, Musketeers, Samurai, Swashbucklers, and Olympic Champions. 2002. Random House. 978-0375504174. 544pp.
    This is a fascinating, fast-paced, yet detailed look at one of man's most enduring weapons—the sword. Many cultures have perfected the blade and created elaborate training rituals and rules of etiquette to accompany its use. Cohen traces the story of the sword from weapon of war through emblem of honor and plaything of gentlemen. He takes detours to discover how swords are made and to tell precisely how they damage a human body. Cohen, himself a British Olympic fencer, obviously loves his subject and shares a vast amount of social history, fact, and anecdote. For more sword story, read *Swords and Swordplay* (2010) by Mike Loades.

Kelly, Jack.
Gunpowder: Alchemy, Bombards, and Pyrotechnics: The History of the Explosive that Changed the World. 2004. Basic Books. 0465037186. 260pp.
    In this easy-reading popular history, Kelly explores the discovery of gunpowder in China and the expansion of its use on battlefields throughout the world. Originally used for magic and fireworks, gunpowder soon became the favored substance for weapons and war. As the technology of weaponry advanced however, gunpowder found itself returned to powering fireworks—a circle that has taken 1,000 years to complete.

Kirk, David.
Child of Vengeance. 2013. Doubleday. 978-0385536639. 336pp. FICTION
    The way of the Samurai dominates this fictional story of the young boy who grows up to be Musashi Miyamoto, author of *The Book of the Five*

Rings—the Japanese classic of martial arts, swordsmanship, and the Samurai ethic. Kirk offers feudal Japan and a coming-of-age story in vivid prose depicting a violent era and showing the evolution of a warrior.

Leebaert, Derek.
To Dare to Conquer: Special Operations and the Destiny of Nations from Achilles to Al Qaeda. 2007. Back Bay Books (paperback). 978-0316014236. 688pp.

Operating deep in hostile territory, using whatever tactics necessary—speed or patience, guile or outright attack, typically inflicting greater damage than they incur, the commandos of history are often overlooked in the larger scope of battle and war. Foreign policy professor Leebaert examines special operations across such diverse theaters of war as Ancient Greece, Conquistadors in America, the Boer War, and Al Qaeda.

Marlantes, Karl.
Matterhorn: A Novel of the Vietnam War. 2010. Atlantic Monthly Press. 978-0802119285. 592pp. FICTION

This recent novel about the Vietnam War compares favorably to such classics as Tim O'Brien's *The Things They Carried* (1990) and Philip Caputo's *A Rumor of War* (1977). Through Marine Second Lieutenant, Ivy League grad, and emerging leader Mellas, we suffer the mundane moments and horrific events that filled this polarizing war. Marlantes includes a "Glossary of Weapons, Technical Terms, Slang, and Jargon" that provides civilian readers an education in Vietnam era warfare and military culture. A powerful, visceral novel.

McLynn, Frank.
Heroes and Villains: Inside the Minds of the Greatest Warriors in History. 2009. Pegasus Books. 978-1605980294. 384pp.

McLynn has written an entertaining compare and contrast showing warrior leaders across time and cultures. Filled with insight into the political strategies and battle tactics of each time and place, McLynn showcases the personalities of these complex and charismatic men, their way of thinking, and their motivations. Spartacus, Attila, Richard the Lionheart, Cortes, Tokugawa, and Napoleon are profiled. Were they brilliantly talented or deeply flawed? Psychopaths or saviors? Champions or mass murderers? Heroes or villains?

McNab, Chris.
▶ ***A History of the World in 100 Weapons.*** 2011. Osprey. 978-1849085205. 384pp.

Arrows, artillery, and atom bombs are all explored as author McNab looks at "history through the prism of military invention." Arranged chronologically with many illustrations and sidebars, this is a fascinating international look at how war and weaponry, though designed to create death and destruction, have always been one of mankind's greatest avenues of innovation and invention. Continue exploring the evolution of weapons with *American Rifle: A Biography*

(2008) by Alexander Rose and *The Gun* (2010) by C. J. Chivers about the evolution of the AK-47.

Sheinkin, Steve.
Bomb: The Race to Build—and Steal—the World's Most Dangerous Weapon. 2012. Roaring Brook Press. 978-1596434875. 266pp. Ⓨ Ⓐ
   Science, technology, espionage, and patriotism, all meet in this book about the race to build and use an atomic bomb. Rapid narrative, fascinating characters like Robert Oppenheimer and a strong sense of story make this a must read. Sheinkin has written this book for young readers, but all fans of 20th-century or military history will be enthralled by the storytelling and can have confidence in Sheinkin's extensive documentation. For a deeper look at the story, read *The Bomb: A Life* (2005) by Gerard J. DeGroot.

Tucker, Jonathan B.
War of Nerves: Chemical Warfare from World War I to Al-Qaeda. 2006. Pantheon. 0375422293. 479pp.
   Tabun, Sarin, VX are chemical killers with no peaceful purpose, death agents that fall outside the realm of "conventional" weapons. Chemical weapons were first deployed during the stalemated trench warfare of World War I. In every military engagement since then, chemical weapons have been a threat and countries continue to produce and test these weapons that no sane nation really wants to use. Tucker details the development of these weapons as well as the dilemma of how to destroy the aging stockpiles that already exist in this sobering look at weapons of mass destruction.

Building Big Things

Engineering and architecture, transportation and communication, in other words, infrastructure. It takes creativity, energy, and gumption to envision a large goal, get others on board, and see the job through to the end. These are the stories of the construction of big things.

Bernstein, Peter L.
▶ *Wedding of the Waters: The Erie Canal and the Making of a Great Nation.* 2005. W. W. Norton. 0393052338. 448pp.
   As early as 1792, plans were underway to connect eastern New York with western New York by water. Thomas Jefferson thought the plan "little short of madness," but in 1825, the Erie Canal opened and American travel, shipping, and commerce was forever changed. Bernstein takes us rapidly through a tour of the world's great canals, and then dives into the story of the conception, creation, and completion of the Erie Canal. Politics, technology, and big personalities merge in this spirited narrative of the first great civic project in America. David McCullough's *The Path between the Seas: The Creation of the Panama Canal, 1870–1914* (1999) tells the compelling story of another famous canal.

Hiltzik, Michael.
Colossus: Hoover Dam and the Making of the American Century. 2010. Free Press. 1416532161. 512pp.

Hoover Dam on the Colorado River at the Nevada and Arizona border is an engineering wonder. Controlling the Colorado River was talked about for years before the dam was finally conceived in the 1920s and built during the darkness of the Great Depression. The result was population expansion in the West, electricity for millions, and a tourist attraction currently visited by more than one million people a year. The site of the dam is majestic. The dam itself is a colossus of concrete and turbines, a work suffused with artistic touches from its Art Deco turrets to its Native American motifs, and a monument to the skill and fortitude of the men who built it. Hiltzik looks at the politics, money, engineering, and general fortitude that allowed the Hoover Dam to be built.

Jonnes, Jill.
Eiffel's Tower: And the World Fair Where Buffalo Bill Beguiled Paris, Artists Quarreled, and Thomas Edison Became a Count. 2009. Viking. 0670020605. 368pp.

Belle Époque France and Gilded Age America met in Paris at the 1889 Exposition where the centerpiece was Gustav Eiffel's engineering marvel, the Eiffel Tower. In the planning stages, the "odious column of bolted metal" inspired fear, hatred, lawsuits, and derision; but once completed, the tower was lauded as a new symbol of France. Jonnes is the author of another book about a great building, *Conquering Gotham: A Gilded Age Epic: The Construction of Penn Station and It's Tunnels* (2007).

King, Ross.
Brunelleschi's Dome: How a Renaissance Genius Reinvented Architecture. 2000. Walker & Company. 978-0802713667. 192pp.

In 1418, a competition was announced in Florence, Italy, to finish construction of the dome of the city's cathedral—a design and engineering dilemma that seemingly had no solution. Enter Filippo Brunelleschi, goldsmith, architect, engineer, and genius whose solution, though it took 20 years to enact, has lasted for 600 years. This is a lively portrait of Renaissance Florence, the rivalry of artists, and civic engineering. For more European splendor, read *Universe of Stone: A Biography of Chartres Cathedral* (2008) by Phillip Ball and *Basilica: The Splendor and the Scandal: Building St. Peters* (2006) by R.A. Scotti.

Swift, Earl.
The Big Roads: The Untold Story of the Engineers, Visionaries and Trailblazers Who Created the American Superhighways. 2011. Houghton Mifflin Harcourt. 978-0618812417. 375pp.

The American Interstate Highway System is an epic achievement—47,000 miles of road, 55,000 bridges, and an array of tunnels and turnpikes at a cost of $130 billion over years of construction. Before this network of roads connected all parts of the country, travelers had to contend with misdirection, danger, and lots and lots of mud. As the interstates were finished, truckers and motorists gained increased safety and greater access to America, but local, regional color began to fade. Earl Swift takes a relaxed tone but a scholarly approach to tell the story of America's highways.

Vogel, Steve.
The Pentagon: A History: The Untold Story of the Wartime Race to Build the Pentagon—and to Restore It Sixty Years Later. 2007. Random House. 978-1400063031. 626pp.

Early in 1941, America was ramping up for war. One thing hampered the effort—the inefficient dispersal of war department employees in office buildings and warehouses throughout Washington D.C. The solution? Create a new building to house all the personnel and leaders needed to wage war. Construction on the world's largest office building was quickly underway. From design to occupancy took less than 18 months. The challenges of creating such a unique building, of working in it, renovating it, and repairing it after the devastating 9/11 attack are all told in exhilarating prose by journalist Vogel.

Wolmar, Christian.
Blood, Iron and Gold: How the Railroads Transformed the World. 2011. Public Affairs (paperback). 978-1586489496. 432pp.

Exploring the building of railroad systems in several countries around the world, Wolmar offers a fascinating account of the social impact and rapid growth of the transportation mode that created new industries, expanded economic and cultural opportunities, and connected people and markets previously out of touch. For more detail about America's railroads, read *Empire Express: Building the First Transcontinental Railroad* (2000) by David Hayward Bain, *Railroaded: The Transcontinentals and the Making of Modern America* (2011) by Richard White, and *Nothing Like It in the World: The Men Who Built the Transcontinental Railroad 1863–1869* (2000) by Stephen E. Ambrose.

Then I Didn't Feel So Well—Microbes that Made History

Throughout history, one of mankind's greatest enemies has been disease. The personal suffering and the heroic search for cures make compelling reading.

Brennert, Alan.
Moloka'i. 2004 (originally published in 2003). St. Martin's Griffin (paperback). 978-0312304355. 416pp. FICTION

Seven-year-old Rachel is growing up happy and carefree in Hawaii in the late 1800s. When it is discovered that she has leprosy like her beloved Uncle

Pono, she is sent to the quarantine colony on the island of Moloka'i to grow up removed from her family and the normal experiences of life that any young girl desires. Gone are her dreams of travel and adventure, instead she faces a life of medical treatments and the frequent heartbreak of seeing friends die. Rachel's story covers the years when medical understanding of Hansen's disease expanded and personal prejudices and fear of the disease declined. A powerful and heartfelt story with a unique setting.

Brooks, Geraldine.
Year of Wonders: A Novel of the Plague. 2001. Penguin (paperback). 978-0142001431. 308pp. FICTION
Elegantly written and filled with vivid detail and tremendous emotion, this is the story of plague that descended on a remote English village in 1666 and the decision the inhabitants made to quarantine themselves so the pest would not spread to neighboring villages. Told through the forthright narration of observant Anna, this is a memorable story that shows how fear and disease can put social order, love, and faith on trial.

Fenn, Elizabeth A.
Pox Americana: The Great Smallpox Epidemic of 1775–82. 2001. Hill and Wang. 978-0809078219. 370pp.
Except for stored vials in two known repositories, the world today is free of smallpox, but America from 1775 to 1782 was overcome with the virus that causes fever, body encasing blisters, and either agonizing death or lifelong immunity. Fenn traces the journey of the disease across the great expanse of the American landscape from the colonies to the Pacific Northwest and from Canada to the Mexican border in this expansive medical history that is also about early America, Native populations, exploration, inoculation, and revolution.

Hayden, Deborah.
Pox: Genius, Madness and the Mysteries of Syphilis. 2003. Basic Books. 0465028810. 379pp.
Hayden takes a mainly biographical approach in this history of syphilis. From the 1500s to the mid-20th century when penicillin arrived to curtail its spread and effect, syphilis was prevalent in the European population and feared by anyone who was sexually active. Hayden tells the stories of creative artists like Karen Blixen and Charles Baudelaire who were known to have the disease, and she speculates that many others from Abraham Lincoln to Adolf Hitler were also sufferers. A fascinating examination of a disease that has been surrounded by secrecy and shame for 500 years.

Johnson, Steven.
The Ghost Map: The Story of London's Most Terrifying Epidemic—And How It Changed Science, Cities, and the Modern World. 2006. Riverhead. 1594489254. 299pp.

The recycling of waste is a process undertaken by all biological life on earth. In London in 1854, that process was in crisis. At the time, London was a burgeoning Victorian city with an Elizabethan infrastructure; there was no system in place for consistent, citywide sanitation. Where sanitary removal of sewage does not happen, cholera—a disease transmitted by human waste—can erupt. And that is what happened in one neighborhood in London in 1854 when the drinking water became contaminated. Johnson successfully incorporates strands of history, biography, science, and medical detection into this compassionate and compelling story.

Keane, Mary Beth.
Fever. 2013. Scribner. 978-1451693416. 306pp. FICTION
    Linked forever are typhoid fever and Mary Mallon, known to the world as Typhoid Mary. An asymptomatic carrier of the disease, Mallon was believed to be responsible for multiple deaths. Mary worked in New York in the early 1900s as a talented cook and sometimes nurse—perfect avenues for spreading infection. Refusing to remove herself from contact with the public, Mary spent the last 23 years of her life as the "special guest" of New York, quarantined, sequestered, and imprisoned to preserve public health. Keane offers a sympathetic and touching look at the woman, the times, and the disease.

Mukherjee, Siddhartha. ♛
Emperor of All Maladies: A Biography of Cancer. 2010. Harper Collins 978-1439107959. 592pp.
    For 4,000 years, almost all of recorded history, humanity has documented this "grotesque and multifaceted illness," and even well into the 20th century, cancer was a word that was whispered because of the fear it invoked. This is a large and absorbing look at the biological, medical, culture, and metaphorical life of cancer. Mukherjee, a practicing oncologist, is an intelligent and supremely humane guide to this malady that isn't "caught" but that grows within a body when cells that should behave one way start to behave another. It is winner of the 2011 Pulitzer Prize for nonfiction.

Oshinsky, David M. ♛
Polio: An American Story: The Crusade that Mobilized the Nation against the 20th Century's Most Feared Disease. 2005. Oxford. 978-0195152944. 342pp.
    Killing some, crippling others, and effecting children most dramatically, polio struck with no warning and caused widespread dread in 20th-century America. This is not only the story of a disease but also of the public relations and scientific battles waged against it. It is also the tale of the bitter rivalry between the brilliant scientists Jonas Salk and Albert Sabin who developed competing vaccines. Oshinsky has delivered a great social and medical history about America in the 20th century and a social campaign to understand and eradicate a disease.

Talty, Stephan.
The Illustrious Dead: The Terrifying Story of How Typhus Killed Napoleon's Greatest Army. 2009. Crown. 978-0307394040. 315pp.

Napoleon invaded Russia with 440,000 frontline troops; by November 1812, only 75,000 remained—disease had killed more men than battle. Typhus—transported by the common body louse—could strike wherever people gathered. A marching army, dirty, hungry, tired, with lowered resistance made a welcome host and Napoleon's men were infested. Lice would happily travel on human carriers hidden in hair and clothing and always ready to move on to and destroy new victims. Talty dramatically mixes medical and military history in this engrossing story about the downfall of an army at the mercy of a little louse.

Wasik, Bill and Monica Murphy.
▶ *Rabid: A Cultural History of the World's Most Diabolical Virus.* 2012. Viking. 978-0670023738. 240pp.

For most of history, the bite of a mad animal has meant certain death to humans. Even today, with advanced knowledge and medical care, rabies is one of mankind's most deadly foes. Though incidences are infrequent, they generally result in an agonizing death. Wasik and Murphy trace the justified fear and the great exaggerations (vampires, werewolves, and zombies) that have surrounded this pathogen. They also explore the heroism of scientists and doctors who have fought it, like Louis Pasteur and his assistants who created a vaccine and modern doctors who use every available means to aid the stricken.

How Money Gets Made (and Lost)

People are endlessly interested in what money is and how to get more of it. These titles offer a look at business and wealth in the past.

Chancellor, Edward.
Devil Take the Hindmost: A History of Financial Speculation. 1999. Farrar Strauss Giroux. 978-0374138585. 386pp.

Optimism and human folly are two themes of Edward Chancellor's very readable book about the international history of financial speculation. Starting from earliest beginnings in Ancient Rome, Chancellor examines numerous famous financial "bubbles": the Mississippi bubble and the South Sea bubble, the Dutch Tulip mania of the 1630s, and technological advances that promised riches, like railways in mid-19th-century Britain. Chancellor does not overwhelm with economic jargon and technical financial details, but fills his book with historical anecdotes and the lively personalities that schemed, plotted, and hoped to get rich.

Delderfield, R.
God Is an Englishman. 2009 (first published in 1970). Sourcebooks (paperback). 978-1402218217. 656pp. FICTION

Adam Swann, lately of the Queen's forces in India, returns to England with the foundations of a fortune and the drive to succeed in a new business—hauling and carting goods to places the new and expanding railroads have passed by. Along the way, he acquires a wife and an entourage of business associates who help him succeed. This business story wrapped in a family saga and set in Industrial Age Britain is an enduring read. This is the first in a trilogy of books that were best sellers in the 1970s. Follow up with *Theirs Was the Kingdom* and *Give Us This Day*.

Dolin, Eric Jay.
Fur, Fortune and Empire: The Epic History of the Fur Trade in America. 2010. Norton. 978-0393067101. 442pp.

To understand American history, you must understand the fur trade, argues Dolin. From Henry Hudson forward, those who came to America understood and exploited the value in the pelts of the abundant native fauna, particularly the beaver, the sea otter, and finally, the buffalo. Dolin creates a masterful work of history and entertaining narrative that looks at the economic and social reality of making a fortune in the fur trade. His energetic writing includes a look at the mountain men and traders who expanded America. Dolin's latest book is *When America First Met China: An Exotic History of Tea, Drugs, and Money in the Age of Sail* (2012).

Donovan, Tristan.
Replay: The History of Video Games. 2010. Yellow Ant. 978-0956507204. 516pp.

This lively read about the inception, growth, and yet-to-come maturation of the video game industry is engaging and unexpected. Donovan, a British journalist, argues that the future is still happening in this 60-year-old industry that has yet to reach a middle-age slump. His story romps from ENIAC to Pac Man to Tetris, Super Mario Brothers and beyond as he covers the personalities and trends in the development and growth of this international industry. It includes a gameography and a hardware glossary.

Hobhouse, Henry.
Seeds of Wealth: Four Plants that Made Men Rich. 2004. Counterpoint. 978-1593760441. 272pp.

The social, moral, and economic impact of four plants that became international commodities—timber, grapes, rubber, and tobacco—is offered in this brief book of narrative essays. How these botanical wonders were discovered and exploited to the benefit of some and the detriment of others makes a fascinating international story told in the elegant prose of British author Hobhouse. Hobhouse also wrote *Seeds of Change: Six Plants that Transformed Mankind* (2005) about cotton, quinine, potatoes, sugar, cocoa, and tea.

Morris, Charles R.
▶ *The Tycoons: How Andrew Carnegie, John D. Rockefeller, Jay Gould, and J.P. Morgan Invented the American Supereconomy.* 2005. Time Books. 978-0805075991. 400pp.

Sheer intelligence, absolute ambition, and personal forcefulness, plus uncanny timing and a convergence of societal, political, and economic forces allowed a handful of men to dominate the world of industry and finance in the last half of the 19th century. After the Civil War, America was ripe for economic expansion. Railroads and mining, steel and oil, manufacturing, new technologies, foreign investment, and the nascent consumer culture were all ready to explode with profit. Carnegie who could be "repellently smarmy," Rockefeller full of "quiet charisma," Gould with his supple business mind but a dark reputation, and Morgan outgoing and "raffish" but a natural disciplinarian who created rules and boundaries for the others to follow were there to take advantage. Their personalities and business machinations created the financial world we still operate in. Morris is witty and opinionated and offers a large view of the growing American economy from the end of the Civil War to the Gilded Age. *The Associates: Four Capitalists Who Created California* (2007) by Richard Rayner is a good companion book.

Parker, Matthew.
The Sugar Barons: Family, Corruption, Empire, and War in the West Indies. 2011. Walker and Company. 978-0802717443. 446pp.

The "course of history, the fate of empires, and the lives of millions" would all be affected by a commodity grown on a chain of steamy tropical islands in the Caribbean Sea—sugar. Sugar from the West Indies was the 17th- and 18th-century equivalent of oil—a valuable product from a nascent industry that attracted the attention of all the great powers of the world. The history of sugar is not sweet and Parker addresses the brutality inherent in this arduous industry (the actual growing and processing of the sugar was very dangerous) where white colonizers could make unimaginable fortunes and secure family wealth for generations, even as they created an economy where buccaneering, slavery, and ruthlessness were the norm.

Robins, Nick.
The Corporation that Changed the World: How the East India Company Shaped the Modern Multinational. 2006. Pluto Press. 978-0745325231. 224pp.

Globalization is not a new phenomenon. Back when news sailed slowly around the world, the British East India Company became the first multinational corporation. From 1600 to 1874, the "Honorable Company" made money for its shareholders, imported goods for its customers, brought glory and revenue to its country, and employed thousands of clerks, traders, sailors, and warehousemen. It also oppressed local populations in India and the Far East, took opium to China, manipulated political situations for its own benefit, and basically governed the countries where it traded. Robins gives a brisk and well-documented overview of the life and times of the company that created the model for the modern shareholding corporate structure that dominates the commercial world today. Pertinent background reading to contemporary stories like *The Smartest Guys in the Room: The Amazing Rise and Scandalous Fall of Enron* (2003) by Bethany McLean and Peter Elkind or *The Wal-Mart Effect: How the World's Most Powerful Company Really Works—And How It's Transforming the American Economy* (2006) by Charles Fishman.

Weightman, Gavin.
The Frozen Water Trade: A True Story. 2003. Hyperion. 078686740X. 254pp.

Human ingenuity can turn a profit anywhere. Ice cut from frozen New England ponds and lakes, packed into ships, and sent south made a fortune for Frederic Tudor until mechanical refrigeration took over the business in the 1880s. Tudor was able to ship his ice as far as Cuba, Europe, and India. For another great story about a uniquely American business, read *Appetite for America: Fred Harvey and the Business of Civilizing the Wild West—One Meal at a Time* (2010) by Stephen Fried.

Dinner Table History—Food, Feasting, Eating, and Manners

The importance of food and the meal cannot be underestimated when looking at history. Relationships are cemented over the conviviality of meals. Wars are waged over the scarcity or surplus of harvests. Civilizations are defined by what they eat and cultures are shaped by how food is shared, presented, revered, or ignored. Each of these books looks at the intersection of food and history.

Fletcher, Nichola.
Charlemagne's Tablecloth: A Piquant History of Feasting. 2004. St. Martin's. 978-1422395523. 256pp.

The sharing of food—from the grandly ceremonial to the elegantly simple—is the topic of Fletcher's smorgasbord of essays about banquets and feasts. From Kwakiutl people sharing a feast of blubber, to the simplicity of cold, hungry children sharing hot potatoes, to the glory days of medieval excess, Fletcher offers an entertaining, idiosyncratic exploration of the social custom of feasting through history and across cultures. For a more academic and archaeological approach, read *Feast: Why Humans Share Food* (2007) by Martin Jones.

Hesser, Amanda.
The Essential New York Times Cookbook: Classic Recipes for a New Century. 2010. Norton. 978-0393061031. 932pp.

You do not have to be looking for a recipe to be intrigued by this cookbook. Hesser scoured 150 years of the *New York Times* newspaper to compile 1,400 representative recipes from the *Times'* well-known foodies (Craig Claiborne and Mark Bittman) and uncredited contributors. The result is a mouth-watering chronicle of American culinary history filled with the humor and passion of the author as she takes you through each recipe, talks about why she chose it, and shares the results from her test kitchen (she cooked them all!). Read Mark Kurlansky's compilation of rediscovered WPA writings, *The Food of a Younger Land: A Portrait of American Food—Before the National Highway System, Before Chain Restaurants, and Before Frozen Food, When the Nation's Food Was Seasonal* (2009), as a companion book to learn more about real American food.

Kelby, N.M.
White Truffles in Winter. 2012. W.W. Norton. 978-0393079999. 334pp. FICTION

World famous chef Auguste Escoffier is crafting his memoirs, detailing a rich life of service to the art of preparing and presenting food. His wife Delphine is dying, and her only remaining wish is that Escoffier will create a dish named for her as he had for so many other women—Sarah Bernhardt, Queen Victoria, Anna Pavlova, Nellie Melba. Kelby's sensuous story, which details many of Escoffier's dishes, offers a study on the power of both food and love.

Kimball, Christopher.
Fannie's Last Supper: Re-creating One Amazing Meal from Fannie Farmer's 1896 Cookbook. 2010. Hyperion. 978-1401323226. 258pp.

Take a fanciful idea, recreating a Victorian upper-crust dinner party, set it in a restored 19th-century Boston kitchen; factor in the difficulty of procuring a calf's head; stir in a new appreciation for the actual heat of a wood cookstove—a heat so intense the modern-day chef's poly-blend pants start to melt onto her thighs; limit modern appliances (except for refrigeration and hot water in the name of food safety); and you have some of the ingredients of this witty story. Kimball details this dinnertime escapade in a dry and witty voice and includes all 28 recipes. This is a genial read about an extravagant moment in the American gastronomic past, a mini biography of Fannie Farmer, a social history of the American kitchen and of turn-of-the-century Boston, and homage to the adventurous spirits of his 21st-century crew who pulled off the feast.

Krondl, Michael.
Sweet Invention: A History of Dessert. 2011. Chicago Review Press. 978-1556529542. 418pp.

Man does not live by potatoes, rice, salt, and fish alone; he needs dessert! Sweetness is one of the tastes all humans crave and desire for it is hardwired into mankind, but dessert is cultural. Taking the basics of sweet—sugar, nuts, fruit and honey, refined flour, butter, cream, and chocolate—and crafting them into works of art to be served to kings is a story with a past and Krondl takes us to India, the Middle East, Italy, France, Austria, and America to explore it. From baklava to Sacher Torte, history is on every dessert plate.

Shapiro, Laura.
Something from the Oven Reinventing Dinner in 1950s America. 2004. Viking.
978-0670871544. 336pp.

    After World War II, the food industry—a relative newcomer on the American business scene and just recently released from feeding troops—took aim on the home cook, "envisioning a day when virtually all contact between the cook and the raw makings of dinner would be obsolete." The explosion of packaged food products aided by marketing innovations like the Pillsbury Bake Off had begun and American kitchens, family dynamics, and waistlines changed. Shapiro tells the stories of several of the mid-century personalities who helped liberate women from the kitchen with their writing and humor. Also read Laura Shapiro's *Perfection Salad: Women and Cooking at the Turn of the Century* (1986).

Standage, Tom.
▶ *A History of the World in Six Glasses.* 2005. Walker and Co. 978-0802714473.
311pp.

    Although water is humanity's basic drink, this enjoyable narrative argues that six other liquids—beer, wine, spirits, coffee, tea, and Coca-Cola—beyond serving as symbols and means of celebration have each contributed to the development of civilizations and cultures, trade and technology, medicine and religion, philosophy, and politics. Standage is a clever and cordial historian and his books are effortless reads that cover a lot of territory and leave you feeling well informed. Also enjoy Standage's *An Edible History of Humanity* (2010).

Tannahill, Reay.
Food in History. 1995 (revised edition, originally published in 1973). Broadway.
978-0517884041. 448pp.

    A panoramic view of a huge subject, written with verve and good humor, and aimed at the average intelligent reader is Tannahill's own summation of her accomplishment. This is a wide-ranging global history about what humanity eats and how we gather, grow, and cook our food. Tannahill is acknowledged as the first author to attempt a comprehensive overview of the history of food and one of the first scholars to stress the importance of food as a subject for historical study. Since the original publication of this volume, the subject of food has become an academic field and a publishing bonanza. For an exploration of the technology of the kitchen, read *Consider the Fork: How Technology Transforms the Way We Cook and Eat* (2012) by Bee Wilson.

Animal, Vegetable, and Mineral—
Microhistories

In recent years, a new way of looking at history has emerged. Called microhistories, these books take an in-depth look at one subject—an event, an item, or a moment. Fun to read, often surprising, these books take unpredictable turns and pull you through time and space in unexpected ways. One of the foremost authors in this genre is Mark Kurlansky, after you have read his narrative masterpieces *Salt* (2003) and *Cod* (1998) move on to these microhistories that explore the big impact of seemingly simple things.

Freese, Barbara.
Coal: A Human History. 2004. Basic Books. 978-0738204000. 320pp.

Think of it as compressed and stored sunlight, coal is the dirty fuel that has benefitted and bedeviled humanity for 2,000 years. Once man learned to dig it from the ground and use it to heat his home and propel his industries, coal became a major player in the history of humanity. These fossilized remains of ancient trees have made some people sick and some people rich. Freese looks at the science of coal, then turns attention to the history of coal focusing on Great Britain and America, and looks at coal's future through the experiences of China.

Hoare, Philip. ♛
The Whale: In Search of the Giants of the Sea. 2010. Ecco. 978-0061976216. 464pp. YA

The mysterious, magical, and monstrous whale inhabits a special place in the psyche of humanity—largest animal on the planet, a mammal that lives not on land with the rest of us but in the ocean, supremely free to roam the planet, hunted but also revered. Hoare has had a long fascination with whales and he uses his considerable skills as a researcher and writer to tell of his passion, exploration, and understanding of these great beasts—their history, science, interactions with man, and place in literature and myth. *Rats: Observations on the History and Habitat of the City's Most Unwanted Inhabitants* (2004) by Robert Sullivan, *Pigeons: The Fascinating Saga of the World's Most Revered and Reviled Bird* (2006) by Andrew Blechman, and *The Tiger: A True Story of Vengeance and Survival* (2010) by John Vaillant are more engrossing animal microhistories.

Koeppel, Dan.
Banana: The Fate of the Fruit that Changed the World. 2007. Hudson Street Press. 978-1594630385. 304pp. YA

Multiple types of bananas are eaten around the world, but in America, we basically only eat one—the Cavendish. This sweet, comforting fruit so easily fed to babies and mashed up for the infirm has a shady past and an uncertain future. Exotic locations, cutting-edge genetic science, cutthroat business deals, and foreign policy created to insure corporate profits (you've heard the term "Banana Republic") are all a part of the banana's past. The uncertain future looms in the form of Panama disease, a rapidly travelling fungus that already wiped out the Cavendish's cousin, the banana our grandparents ate, the Gros Michel. Koeppel tells the banana's story with passion, humor, and clarity.

Lockwood, Jeffrey Alan.

Locust: The Devastating Rise and Mysterious Disappearance of the Insect that Shaped the American Frontier. 2004. Basic Books. 978-0756797652. 294pp.

The Rocky Mountain locust, North American's only locust, was once a player in the settling of the West. At various times, in the late 1800s, trillions, yes trillions, of the long legged, wide-winged insects swarmed the Great Plains blacking out the sun, decimating crops, horrifying settlers, stopping trains on their tracks, and leaving behind mountains of stinking locusts carcasses. But the Rocky Mountain locust exists no more and has been gone from the American scene since 1902, the final recorded outbreak. Lockwood sets out to discover why this creature disappeared. His account of the devastation the locust caused, the terror of the swarms, and his own biological detective work to unravel the reasons the locusts disappeared is a history lesson written like an eco-thriller.

Logan, William Bryant.

▶ *Oak: The Frame of Civilization.* 2005. Norton & Company. 978-0393047738. 320pp.

Oak trees are prevalent across the temperate regions of the world. From mythology to art, commerce, and design, their strength and enduring stability have been prized. Oaks have provided man with the material to create a good life: food in the form of acorns, protection in its strong base and spreading branches, and wood for building ships of discovery, houses of stolid comfort, boxes for safekeeping treasures, and barrels for storing and shipping provisions (the author estimates that in medieval Europe, there were more oak barrels than people). Logan's easy prose moves gracefully through the story of the oak tree—other trees are bigger, older, stronger, but the oak has been a partner to mankind throughout history.

Shah, Sonia.

Crude: The Story of Oil. 2004. Seven Stories Press. 1583226257. 232pp.

In smooth prose and broad strokes, Shah tells the history of crude oil from its early discovery as mysterious flames spouting in the Arabian desert—giving rise to Zoroastrian worship—through Rockefeller's exploration to the manipulations of today's geopolitical cartels. A brief, very readable history that provides needed background for some of today's pressing questions: who controls the oil, how much is left, and what will we do when it is all gone? Shah is also the author of *The Fever: How Malaria Has Ruled Humankind for 500,000 Years* (2010).

The Crime of the Century— Yesterday's True Crime Stories

The gold standard for historical true crime that mixes in plenty of social history is Erik Larson's best seller *The Devil in the White City: Murder, Magic, and*

Madness at the Fair that Changed America (2003). Since its success, readers have wanted more crimes set in the past. These books set crime in the context of an era and show that law enforcement, criminal science, investigative techniques, and legal procedures may have changed, but human nature never does.

Blum, Deborah.
The Poisoner's Handbook: Murder and the Birth of Forensic Medicine in Jazz Age New York. 2010. Penguin. 978-1594202438. 336pp.

> The chemical realm of modern American forensic science is explored through the lives and scientific work of New York medical examiner Charles Norris and toxicologist Alexander Gettler. Through tales of murder and misadventure, Blum details the specific properties of several poisons and illuminates their effect on victims. This is a ghoulish but riveting exploration of poison and poisoners and of the men who ended the era of the perfect, undetectable crime.

Burrough, Bryan.
Public Enemies: America's Greatest Crime Wave and the Birth of the FBI, 1933–1934. 2004. Penguin. 978-1594200212. 592pp.

> Making extensive use of FBI files released "in bits and pieces" since the mid-1980s and writing in a colorful, documentary style, Burroughs enters the1930s to depict the outlaws who ran wild and the federal government's response to their deeds. J. Edgar Hoover—depicted as brilliant, but strange—is the centerpiece of the story as he restructures the FBI to become the country's national police force. Working with him are the G-men heroes who battled to make America (or at least the money in the banks) safe from criminals like Bonnie and Clyde, Dillinger, Ma Barker, Alvin "Creepy" Karpis, and Pretty Boy Floyd.

Faye, Lyndsay.
Gods of Gotham: A Novel. 2012. Putnam. 0399158375. 432pp. FICTION

> Faye sets her convincing thriller in vivid New York City in 1845 just as Irish immigrants are pouring into the city and a new police force is being created. Bartender Timothy Wilde joins the new force and gets a beat near the notorious Five Points area. Just as he starts his new profession, Wilde is pulled into a mystery when a frantic little girl tells him a tale of bodies buried in the nearby woods. Faye is a masterful new writer. Her first book is *Dust and Shadows* (2009) in which Sherlock Holmes meets Jack the Ripper.

O'Brien, Geoffrey.
▶ *The Fall of the House of Walworth: A Tale of Madness and Murder in Gilded Age America.* 2010. Henry Holt. 978-0805081152. 337pp.

> An engrossing story of the Walworth family of Saratoga Springs, New York, a redoubtable family who participated in New York State history since their American arrival in 1680. But a streak of strangeness flowed through the family and it came to a crisis when scion of the clan, Mansfield Walworth—author of second-rate potboiler dime novels, father of eight children, and chronic wife

abuser—finally threatened to kill the mother of his children. The story begins when Frank Walworth, Mansfield's eldest son, steps in to protect his mother and bring his father's reign of terror to a close. This lurid family scandal, crime, trial, and aftermath is set in the moody Gothic atmosphere of a creepy family mansion and played out on the fringes of Gilded Age New York.

Pomerantz, Gary.
The Devil's Tickets: A Night of Bridge, a Fatal Hand, and a New American Age. 2009. Crown. 978-1400051625. 300pp.

The marriages of couples that play contract bridge seem to end badly, some in messy public divorces and some in murder. Social history and crime story combine in this hard-to-put-down story about Ely Culbertson who popularized the card game with his wife Jo in the 1920s and the parallel story of the fatal effect a bad hand of bridge had on one couple in Kansas City, Missouri, in 1929.

Raab, Selwyn.
Five Families: The Rise, Decline, and Resurgence of America's Most Powerful Mafia Empires. 2005. Thomas Dunne Books. 978-0312300944. 765pp.

In the 20th century, five prominent New York–based, Italian American families—Bonanno, Colombo, Gambino, Genovese, and Lucchese—ruled the best coordinated, most powerful, and wealthiest underworld operations in American crime employing intimidating characters like "Fat Pete," "Big Paul," and "Matty the Horse" and profiting from bootlegging, prostitution, protection rackets, construction fraud, and control of the entire New York City waste disposal business. Raab covers the Mafia's history from beginnings in Sicily to its oft times vicious expression in 20th-century New York. This is a fast-paced telling with great attention to detail, written with journalistic verve by a former *New York Times* crime reporter.

Rayner, Richard.
A Bright and Guilty Place: Murder, Corruption, and L.A.'s Scandalous Coming of Age. 2009. Doubleday. 0385509707. 288pp.

Explore the sordid and seamy noir world of Los Angeles where the lawyers, cops, and politicians were as bad as the pimps, gangsters, and swindlers; and all of them were making money from the overflow of wealth in the 1920s and early 1930s. Silent film-star Clara Bow, E. L. Doheny one of L.A.'s founding citizens, and chroniclers like Raymond Chandler, Erle Stanley Gardner, and James M Cain, all make guest appearances in this recounting of a time when Los Angeles was so corrupt that City Hall and the criminal underworld worked as one. Rayner, a British ex-pat who has adopted L.A. as his home, writes in hard-boiled, rapid-fire prose perfectly suited to his material.

Starr, Douglas.
The Killer of Little Shepherds: A True Crime Story and the Birth of Forensic Science. 2010. Knopf. 978-0307266194. 320pp.

In France, at the end of the 19th century, a serial killer is working his way through the countryside viciously slaughtering young people. Meanwhile, in Lyon, scientist, doctor, criminologist, and professor Alexandre Lacassagne is working to codify criminal science into a system that can be used by police, medical examiners, lawyers, and all those concerned with bringing criminals to justice and seeing that the innocent remain free. Abjuring torture, hunches, bias, and superstition, Lacassagne along with his students and colleagues helped create the groundwork for the science of criminology. Starr tells a fascinating story of the beginnings of criminal forensics—footprints, blood-spatter, autopsy best practices, crime scene investigation, profiling, and interdepartmental communication.

Stashower, Daniel.
The Beautiful Cigar Girl: Mary Rogers, Edgar Allan Poe, and the Invention of Murder. 2006. Dutton. 052594981X. 326pp.

Beautiful young Mary Rogers, formerly a cigar girl in a store in New York, was brutally killed in 1841. Her death sparked an explosion of newspaper rivalries and initiated a rethinking of the effectiveness of the New York City police department. Edgar Allan Poe used the basic facts of her unsolved murder to write his story "The Mystery of Marie Roget"—his second detective story featuring the master of ratiocination, amateur detective C. Auguste Dupin. This mesmerizing book is part crime story, part New York history, part Poe biography, and part literary analysis of one of the earliest and most famous mystery stories.

All Work and No Play—The History of Fun and Games

History isn't only kings and queens, wars and disasters, revolutions and political upheavals. How humanity has just passed its time is also worthy of study. Learn a little about the history of fun in these books about sports and games.

Maraniss, David.
Rome 1960: The Olympics that Changed the World. 2008. Simon & Schuster 978-0641989346. 496pp.

Every four years, the world convenes to witness the most elite athletes compete at the Olympics. In 1960, the meeting in Rome became a turning point bringing the Olympics into the modern world of televised coverage, sponsorship, doping, increased integration, and the looming Cold War. Journalist Maraniss offers an expansive narrative of the international gathering where Cassius Clay became a star, Wilma Rudolph blazed across the track, and Rafer Johnson brought home gold in the decathlon.

McManus, James.
   Cowboys Full: The Story of Poker. 2009. FSG. 0374299242. 528 pp.
   Spirited and wide-ranging, this history of poker is also a history of the American character. Although the Founding Fathers didn't play poker as we know it and the game was still evolving in their era, this card game that is a really a psychological contest of strategy, patience, and bluffing eventually permeated American politics and culture. Lincoln joked about poker, Nixon funded his first congressional campaign with poker winnings, and Eisenhower won so much off fellow soldiers that he quit playing out of fairness. For a lively look at the broader story of gambling, read *Roll the Bones: A History of Gambling* (2006) by David Schwartz.

Orbanes, Philip.
   Monopoly: The World's Most Famous Game. 2007. Da Capo Press. 978-0306814891. 262pp.
   From its roots as the *Landlord's Game*, intended to teach college students about economics, rents, and, well, monopolies, *Monopoly* became the all-time best-selling board game and a common theme in the childhood of most Americans. Orbanes, himself a judge at the World Monopoly Tournaments, tells the origins and growth of a board game that could only happen in America where a woman named Elizabeth Magie Phillips invented a game about trust busting and financial reform. Once the Parker Brothers—New England entrepreneurs who owned the largest game making company in America—entered the picture, the rest, as they say, is history.

Shenk, David.
   ▶ *The Immortal Game: A History of Chess.* 2007. Anchor. 978-1400034086. 352pp.
   Shenk tells the story of the 1,500-year-old thinking tool that masquerades as a game played by kings, school children, and computers. Chess is one of the few games whose rules have survived almost unchanged since its inception. It has successfully traveled across cultures as diverse as India and medieval Europe to our own era of technology and artificial intelligence. It is a game that changes the brain and has perhaps led to madness in some players. For more good reads about chess, try *Endgame: Bobby Fischer's Remarkable Rise and Fall—From America's Brightest Prodigy to the Edge of Madness* (2011) by Frank Brady and *Birth of the Chess Queen: A History* (2005) by Marilyn Yalom.

Thompson, Neal.
   Driving with the Devil: Southern Moonshine, Detroit Wheels, and the Birth of NASCAR. 2006. Crown. 978-1400082254. 411pp.
   The combination of the '39 Ford V-8, backwoods dirt roads, Scots Irish independence, and moonshine added up to one thing—NASCAR. The sport today glosses over its "distant whiskey-fueled origins," but Thompson pro-

vides all the color of the early years, the vibrant personalities, and the evolution of this racing sport that is also a family-owned business.

Vecsey, George.
Baseball: A History of America's Favorite Game. 2008. Modern Library. 978-0812978704. 272pp.

Americans identify with baseball. It permeates our language and our culture. It's a homegrown sport with international roots and appeal. It's a game, a business, a philosophy, and a passion. Vecsey, sports columnist for the *New York Times* and lifelong fan, has crafted a sympathetic and elegantly written overview of America's pastime that touches on the historic moments, the personalities, the triumph, and the heartbreak of this urban game that is played in a ballpark where the players are, in the words of George Carlin, just trying to go home.

Broad Strokes—Books That Span Time

These books offer up big chunks of history, from prehistory to postwar, for readers who want an expansive view of a big piece of the past.

Brown, Cynthia Stokes.
▶ *Big History: From the Big Bang to the Present.* 2007. New Press 978-1595581969. 304pp.

Big History is bigger than World History. The narrative starts with the Big Bang and seeks to explain what was happening on Earth for the 13 billion years before humanity entered the story. It also tries to project the story forward, to what will happen in the far future as the expanding universe continues to expand. Big History offers such a large temporal scale and multidisciplinary view that the brief wanderings of popes and kings, explorers, and artists start to seem inconsequential. Brown is an erudite and compassionate guide for this cosmic approach. For more Big History, read *Maps of Time* (2004) by David Christian.

Cantor, Norman.
Antiquity: The Civilization of the Ancient World. 2003. Harper Collins. 978-0060174095. 256pp.

The late scholar Norman Cantor, an expert in medieval history, offers a primer on the civilizations of antiquity. He traces the story from the dawn of humanity through Ancient Egypt and Greece to the rise of Judaism and Christianity and the fall of Rome. Cantor uses elegant language to explain how these long-gone civilizations continue to influence us today.

Judt, Tony
Postwar: A History of Europe since 1945. 2005. Penguin. 1594200653.878pp.

Explore the political, economic, cultural, and psychological reality of an evolving Europe as it emerged from the shadow of World War II. Judt guides us through monumental postwar events like Scandinavian socialism, Polish solidarity, the spread of "Americanization" abetted by the expansion of media, the international baby boom, Mrs. Thatcher's Britain, and the creation of the European Union. The breadth and detailed content of this book border on overwhelming, but Judt's writing is clear and straightforward making a huge chunk of the recent human story available and engrossing.

MacCulloch, Diarmaid.
The Reformation: A History. 2004. Viking. 978-0670032969. 800pp.

The world from 1490 to 1700 was in upheaval over how to worship and what religion meant. This is a beautiful work that takes a complex time of world crisis and lays out the people, events, issues, and ideas for contemporary readers. MacCulloch writes surprisingly comfortable, friendly prose given the seriousness of the subject. MacCulloch is also the author of *Christianity: The First Three Thousand Years* (2010).

Mithen, Steven.
After the Ice: A Global Human History 20,000–5000 BC. 2006. Harvard. 978-0674019997. 664pp.

Mithen creates a character that wanders silently and unseen through Stone Age encampments observing how our ancient ancestors lived, what they made, ate, hunted, and built. Left with only the rubbish of the past—piles of bones, bits of dwellings, and chips of stone—we rely on the best guesses of archaeologists and scientists for the story of the first 15,000 years of humanity. Mithen's style is scholarly yet friendly, dense but never dry. He lays out evidence and discusses methods for surmising the story of this faraway human past.

Illuminating America

America—melting pot, tapestry, kaleidoscope, and crazy quilt—is a place with a million stories. To find the real America, read these histories that show diverse pieces of the story.

Bailey, John.
The Lost German Slave Girl: The Extraordinary True Story of Sally Miller and Her Fight for Freedom in Old New Orleans. 2003. Grove. 978-0802142290. 288pp.

This book is about many things—slavery, New Orleans, redemptioners, immigrants to America who paid their passage by becoming indentured servants upon their arrival, the law, America in the first half of the 19th century, and a woman who lived as a slave but claimed to be a German immigrant. Other German immigrants who declared they had known her as a child picked up her cause and fought for her freedom. Bailey has captured a moment in American history and written it as a legal thriller set in unique and mysterious New Orleans.

Berkin, Carol.
Revolutionary Mothers: Women in the Struggle for America's Independence.
2005. Alfred A. Knopf. 978-1400041633. 194pp.

While Colonial men fought the American Revolution with guns and cannons, the women, though unarmed, fought too: they boycotted British goods; spied; supported troops with food, clothing, shelter, and medical aid; ransacked cupboards to gather metal for bullets; and put on brave faces saying good-bye to their men while remaining in remote towns and isolated homestead, tending crops, caring for children, and realistically facing rape and death if the British came. Some women even did take up arms. Berkin, a professor of American history, tells the story of the bravery and fortitude of the women of America who endured eight years of a brutal home-front war that ended with the founding of a new nation.

Faust, Drew Gilpin.
This Republic of Suffering: Death and the American Civil War. 2008. Knopf. 978-0375404047. 368pp.

Death became a constant in American society during the Civil War. Battle and disease created previously unimagined numbers of casualties. What to do with the wounded, the dying, and the dead? Embalming, transporting, burying, mourning, and memorializing the fallen became an entire industry and the social, cultural, psychic, economic, and political impact affected generations. Faust offers a unique look at one of the effects of the War Between the States.

Miller, Scott.
The President and the Assassin: McKinley, Terror, and Empire at the Dawn of the American Century. 2011. Random House. 978-1400067527. 422pp.

Popular, affable, even-tempered, and fair-minded McKinley was the first president of the 20th century. Reelected for a second term in 1900 after steering America through the Spanish American War, McKinley fell victim to an assassin in September 1901. More than a story about President McKinley and the anarchist who was his assassin, this is a portrait of America on the verge of becoming a world power.

Rutkow, Eric.
American Canopy: Trees, Forests and the Making of a Nation. 2012. Scribner 978-1439193549. 416pp.

Rutkow offers an enthralling new way to consider the history of America— through its trees. From earliest times, trees sheltered pioneers, hampered expansion, created fortunes, and formed American characters from Johnny Appleseed to Gifford Pinchot to Frederick Weyerhaeuser. At one time, the American forest seemed immeasurable and the number of trees covering the continent uncountable. All that has changed and Rutkow details how in this unusual and eloquent take on the American story.

Wilkerson, Isabel. ♛
The Warmth of Other Suns: The Epic Story of America's Great Migration.
2010. Random House 978-0679444329. 640pp.

Wilkerson uses the personal stories of three individuals to tell the epic story of the Great Migration—the informal and generally undocumented mass movement of African Americans out of the South that took place from 1910 to the 1970s. People moved to California, New York, Chicago, and other points North and West—away from Jim Crow, poll taxes, economic uncertainty, and overt racism. This is a beautifully written book that mixes intimate family stories with large historical moments to illuminate a previously untold part of the American story.

Woodard, Colin.
▶ *American Nations: A History of the Eleven Rival Regional Cultures of North America.* 2011. Viking. 978-0670022960. 371pp.

Woodard offers a compelling case that the United States, far from being a nation of unified people with common interests, is a landmass made up of distinct regional cultures with deep differences that affect economics, politics, education, labor, and commerce. These differences are the remnants of the beliefs and characters of early settlers to each region like stable, educated Yankees who spread West from New England to create Yankeedom; semifeudal aristocratic Cavaliers who founded the Tidewater areas of the upper South; and the inhabitants of El Norte where southwest American states and northern Mexican states first settled by Conquistadors and missionaries have more in common with each other than their own nations. This is a thought-provoking look at the historical basis of our current state of the union.

Chapter Two

Character

Around 108 billion—that is the "highly speculative" and "semiscientific" estimate of the number of people who have ever lived on earth figured by Carl Haub of the Population Reference Bureau. So how many life stories are floating around out there? 108 billion. When you have the perspective of 108 billion, you realize how few life stories have been written down, but those few thousands do make for terrific reading. To follow another human being from birth to death, or through the most dramatic moments of their journey, to see the world as they see it, to take a first-person approach to history is the appeal of character. Straight biography, memoir, and narrative history heavily weighted toward personality all demand our attention and fulfill our need to know the story of another human being.

The lists here include books that are traditional biographies, like the work about Madam C. J. Walker, and narrative histories that feature a moment when the lives of several people intersected and the characters of each were illuminated, like John Wilkes Booth and his conspirators as they fled justice. Included are stories about big brains and creative spirits, and stories about men who made fortunes like Thomas Lipton and women whose positions as queen should have made them powerful but gave them lives filled with sorrow and terror. And even though character naturally implies people, the lives of animals have stories to tell that can illuminate the past, like the life of Zarafa—the lovely celebrity giraffe who lived in Paris in the early 1800s—or beloved Hollywood star Rin Tin Tin.

The delightful, the illustrious, and the unknown share equal billing in these lists. Some of these life stories are familiar and some will be entirely new. All of these books will fascinate you.

Leader of the Free World— The Character of the President

There was a time when biographers wrote only glowing portraits of America's leaders. In recent years, historians have offered fuller portraits of the complex characters and intricate lives of the men who were America's presidents.

Algeo, Matthew.
The President Is a Sick Man: Wherein the Supposedly Virtuous Grover Cleveland Survives a Secret Surgery at Sea and Vilifies the Courageous Newspaperman Who Dared Expose the Truth. 2011. Chicago Review Press. 978-1569763506. 272pp.

> Everyone has secrets, even presidents. Grover Cleveland, a man who campaigned for political office on a platform of total honesty, had several. One secret was his illegitimate son; another secret was a health scare that led to a clandestine surgery. In 1893, Cleveland underwent a covert operation to remove a cancer from his palate. He refused to acknowledge media reports about the operation. Algeo offers a lively look at the economics, politics, and social world of Cleveland's times in this entertaining and informative read about America's 22nd and, since Cleveland was elected to another nonconsecutive term, the 24th president.

D'Este, Carlo.
Eisenhower: A Soldier's Life. 2002. Henry Holt and Company. 0805056866. 848pp.

> Massive, detailed, and insightful, this examination of Dwight D. Eisenhower looks at his life from a poor Midwest childhood to his victory as the Supreme Allied Commander in Europe during World War II. D'Este focuses on the military career, personal and professional relationships, and personality traits—gregarious but remote, ambitious and stubborn, and possessor of a "flaming temper" and "considerable ego"—that contributed to the man who became America's 34th president. D'Este is a renowned and award-winning military historian who has also written about Patton and Churchill.

Flood, Charles Bracelen.
Grant's Final Victory: Ulysses S. Grant's Heroic Last Year. 2011. Da Capo Press. 978-0306820281. 288pp.

> One of the most important and powerful books in the American library is the *Personal Memoirs of Ulysses S. Grant.* The story behind the writing of the

memoirs shows the true character of the man. In 1884, having been defrauded by a business partner, the Grant family was broke and Ulysses was dying of throat cancer. He labored for a year to complete the book he knew would provide an income for his family after his death. Flood offers the life and character of America's 18th president and his last year of sickness and creativity as he struggled to complete his memoirs.

Millard, Candice.
Destiny of the Republic: A Tale of Madness, Medicine, and the Murder of the President. 2011. Doubleday. 978-0385526265. 352pp.

James Garfield was a brief president. He was shot by an assassin in July 1881 after being inaugurated as America's 20th president that March. He lay dying for the final two months of his presidency. Millard offers great insight into James Garfield, a president whose character was noble but whose impact was slight. She also gives readers a panoramic view of America after the Civil War, the (mal)practice of medicine during Garfield's times, and the innovations of the late 19th century (like antiseptic) that perhaps could have saved the life of the president. Another fine presidential book by Millard is *River of Doubt: Theodore Roosevelt's Darkest Journey* (2005).

Rubin, Gretchen.
Forty Ways to Look at JFK. 2005. Ballantine Books. 0345450493. 387pp. 📚

What is it about John F. Kennedy that is endlessly fascinating? His charisma never seems to diminish. In brief chapters, Rubin looks at different aspects of Kennedy's life and mind, character and persona, his ideals, his legacy, and his lies to try to ascertain the enduring magnetism of America's 35th president. For a more conventional biography, read *An Unfinished Life: John F. Kennedy, 1917–1963* (2003) by Robert Dallek.

Shenk, Joshua Wolf.
▶ *Lincoln's Melancholy: How Depression Challenged a President and Fueled His Greatness.* 2005. Houghton Mifflin Harcourt. 978-0618551163. 368pp.

"From a place of trouble he looked for meaning." The eminence of Abraham Lincoln, his achievements, and his fortitude seem even greater when you consider he may have battled clinical depression his entire life. According to Shenk, Lincoln's mental suffering, something many who met Lincoln had remarked upon, never went away, but became a characteristic that fed his greatness: "The suffering he had endured lent him clarity, discipline, and faith in hard times. . . ." A fascinating, well-documented psychological look at America's 16th president.

Wiencek, Henry.
Master of the Mountain: Thomas Jefferson and His Slaves. 2012. Farrar, Straus and Giroux. 978-0374299569. 352pp.

Wiencek offers a portrait of America's third president that focuses on Jefferson's own conflicted attitudes and actions regarding one topic—slavery. Jefferson owned slaves and he profited financially from their labor, how could he espouse liberty and equality yet possess other human beings as property? Wiencek's book has been praised, but also criticized as a one-sided portrayal of a brilliant and complex man. To round out the portrait, read *Thomas Jefferson: The Art of Power* (2012) by Jon Meacham and *The Hemingses of Monticello: An American Family* (2008) by Annette Gordon-Reed.

Theodore Roosevelt—America's Most Energetic President

In American history, from 1858 to 1919, Theodore Roosevelt is everywhere—as a little boy he witnessed Lincoln's funeral procession through New York, he was a cowboy out west, he fomented and fought in the Spanish American War, served as president, went on safari in Africa, explored the Amazon in South America, wrote books, won a Nobel Peace Prize, and saved football. The fullest picture of Roosevelt is found in Edmund Morris's magisterial three-volume biography, but these books each offer a facet of this larger-than-life American.

Brinkley, Douglas.
Wilderness Warrior: Theodore Roosevelt and the Crusade for America. 2009. Harper Collins. 978-0060565282. 940pp.

Teddy Roosevelt loved animals, nature, the Western states, and all of the great outdoors. As president, Roosevelt created national parks and monuments, game preserves, bird reservations, and national forests. He made sure that land was set aside for future generations to study and enjoy. Roosevelt created a dialog among America's naturalists, scientists, academics, and outdoorsmen. Brinkley looks at the life of Roosevelt as the conservationist and outdoor enthusiast in this very comprehensive and engrossing volume. Continue reading about outdoor Roosevelt in Timothy Egan's *The Big Burn: Teddy Roosevelt and the Fire that Saved America* (2009).

Davis, Deborah.
Guest of Honor: Booker T Washington, Theodore Roosevelt, and the White House Dinner that Shocked a Nation. 2012. Atria. 978-1439169810. 308pp.
Y A

Booker T. Washington and Theodore Roosevelt had vastly different lives, but in some ways, their lives were perfectly parallel. Both constantly strove to be better men, learn more, do more, and help others. In 1901, Washington dined at the White House with the First Family—the first African American to ever do so. The tumult that resulted was historic. Davis includes many anecdotes about the lives of both of these men, their families, and the social and political worlds they moved in. This is popular narrative history, easy to read, and memorable; a good introduction to two intriguing Americans and their times.

Kerr, Joan Patterson.
▶ *A Bully Father: Theodore Roosevelt's Letters to His Children.* 1995. Random House. 067943948x. 260pp.

Though often away from his family, Roosevelt communicated to his six rambunctious children through a constant stream of letters that were both personal and fun. Roosevelt connected with children—his wife once referred to him as her "oldest and rather worst child." Whether encouraging or admonishing, relating his exploits, or showing genuine interest in theirs, these letters show Roosevelt as a compassionate and engaged father and friend to his children, a man who was full of warmth and love for his family. Kerr offers a nice introductory essay and many family photographs. To explore Roosevelt's own childhood, read *Mornings on Horseback: The Story of an Extraordinary Family, a Vanished Way of Life and the Unique Child Who Became Theodore Roosevelt* (1981) by David McCullough.

Miller, John J.
The Big Scrum: How Teddy Roosevelt Saved Football. 2011. Harper. 978-0061744506. 272pp.

After receiving the Nobel Peace Prize for his negotiations between Russia and Japan, Theodore Roosevelt next tackled football. Football in 1905, still a relatively new sport, had become dangerous and deadly. Roosevelt, an advocate of the "strenuous life," physical exertion, and the personal confrontation of risk, believed the game worth saving because it offered a (relatively) safe forum where boys became men. President Roosevelt convened a gathering of college football coaches and their meeting resulted in new rules, new standards of play, and the beginnings of the NCAA. Miller tells a great story set in the progressive era where the character of Theodore Roosevelt and the power of the presidency saved football.

Thomas, Evan.
The War Lovers: Roosevelt, Lodge, Hearst, and the Rush to Empire, 1898. 2010. Little, Brown. 978-0316004091. 471pp.

Gilded Age personalities take center stage in this story of the origins and outcomes of the Spanish American War. Theodore Roosevelt, William Randolph Hearst, and Henry Cabot Lodge create a war that profited them all—Hearst sold more newspapers and Roosevelt became a hero destined for the White House. Calmer heads like Harvard professor, philosopher, and early psychologist William James and Speaker of the House Thomas Reed offered contrasting opinions during this time of America's brief foray into imperialism. An excellent evocation of the time and the larger-than-life personalities that propelled America into the international scene.

Zacks, Richard.
Island of Vice: Theodore Roosevelt's Doomed Quest to Clean up Sin-Loving New York. 2012. Doubleday. 978-0385519724. 448pp.

New York in the 1890s was full of sin—saloons serving liquor on Sunday, overt prostitution, opium dens, gambling, pickpockets, crooked cops, and corrupt officials. Enter Theodore Roosevelt, appointed Commissioner of Police in 1895 and charged with cleaning up the police force and the city. Roosevelt was an effective manager, an energetic reformer, and a somewhat overzealous prig who had the drive to clean up the vice even though New Yorkers weren't really interested—New Yorkers wanted to have a grown-up good time. After two years, Roosevelt went on to be Assistant Secretary to the Navy and New Yorkers went back to their fun. Zacks paints a vivid portrait of Gilded Age New York and the personalities who worked with and against Roosevelt in his efforts to sanitize New York—the only mission he ever failed in.

Medieval Lives

The Middle Ages hold a deep fascination for readers. These stories of medieval lives, both well known and unknown, offer a feel for the medieval world.

Baer, Ann.
Down the Common: A Year in the Life of a Medieval Woman. 1998. M. Evans and Co. (paperback). 978-0871318749. 240pp. FICTION

The ordinary life of a peasant woman is imagined in this fictional story that unfolds like an elegant documentary. Marion's life is a cycle of births and deaths, and of plenty and want. The era's ignorance and the general poverty of society combine to create her reality, but so do sunshine, flowers, community, and family. This is a simple, affecting chronicle of a year that portrays the life and the mind of a woman living a simple life of toil, hardship, and small joys in medieval England.

Follett, Ken.
Pillars of the Earth. 1996 (originally published in 1989). Turtleback. 978-1417671687. 992pp. FICTION

Royal maneuvering, religion that is sometimes nurturing and sometimes terrible, and demons both personal and societal converge in the fictional 12th-century English town of Kingsbridge where several characters hope to build a great cathedral. This masterful novel immerses readers in the Middle Ages with its large cast of characters, family drama, political intrigue, and well-crafted setting. Prolific author Follett published *World without End* in 2007 set in the same town 200 years later when the Black Death strikes.

Goldstone, Nancy.
Four Queens: The Provençal Sisters Who Ruled Europe. 2007. Penguin. 978-0143113256. 336pp.

Four beautiful and accomplished sisters from elegant and sunny Provence, Marguerite, Eleanor, Blanche, and Sanchia were not born royal, but each went on to become a queen and to influence the politics of 13th-century Europe. Their lives were lived on the largest stage possible for a medieval woman, and their story is fresh and intriguing, told with much style by popular historian Goldstone. If you like authors Philippa Gregory, Alison Weir, and Antonia Fraser, add Goldstone to your reading list.

Jones, Terry.

▶ *Terry Jones' Medieval Lives.* 2007. BBC. 978-0563487937. 256pp. Y̲ A̲
Yes, Monty Python's Terry Jones is an author and a student of history in his off-screen life. His goal in this volume was to strip away the Renaissance biases and Victorian romanticism that have mythologized the medieval world and show how people lived in the broad time span that we call medieval and he defines as 1066–1536. In light-hearted, anecdotal prose, Jones looks at the layers of society—peasant, minstrel, outlaw, monk, philosopher, knight, damsel, and king—to show what life must have been like across medieval society. Jones has also written about the Crusades and the barbarians.

Reston, James.

Warriors of God: Richard the Lionheart and Saladin in the Third Crusade. 2001. Doubleday. 978-0385495615. 384pp.
Two of the most spectacular personalities of the Middle Ages were Saladin and Richard the Lionheart, world leaders and combatants during the Third Crusade (1189–1192). Each man supplied a heroic ideal of courage and right action for their followers and an outsized focus of hatred to their enemies. Reston offers a spirited look at the deeds and times of these two larger-than-life men of history.

Spoto, Donald.

Reluctant Saint: The Life of Francis of Assisi. 2002. Viking. 0670031283. 257pp.
A young man from a wealthy Italian family forsakes the indulgent life his family's wealth provides to walk in poverty and humility doing God's work on earth. Francis (1181–1226) evolved from playboy and solider to penitent and saint, to become a spiritual leader who expressed a simple, spontaneous, and joyful faith marked by compassion and submission, love of nature and animals, gentleness, and acceptance of all God's creatures. His spirit captivated medieval followers. Spoto, best known as a Hollywood biographer, offers a portrait of a man whose different way of thinking made him a celebrity for his times.

Tuchman, Barbara. ♛

A Distant Mirror: The Calamitous 14th Century. 1987 (originally published in 1978). Ballantine (paperback). 978-0345349576. 704pp.
Tuchman's 1978 classic creates a panoramic view of the medieval world of France and Britain by following the life of one man, Enguerrand de Coucy.

Tuchman chose him because he was neither a king nor a peasant, but a well-connected knight and a soldier involved in the great issues and battles of his time. She offers not a strict biography, but an examination of an age with de Coucy as her narrative center. Tuchman uses details and specifics to illuminate the tumultuous 14th century, an era of violence and upheaval, rapid change, and "collapsing assumptions"—an era in many ways, Tuchman argues, like our own.

Conquerors and Kings

These men played large roles in history, because whether by birth or by force they became rulers, leaders, and commanders. Through brilliance, stupidity, cunning, or luck, each affected the world.

Carter, Miranda.
George, Nicholas and Wilhelm: Three Royal Cousins and the Road to World War I. 2010. Knopf. 1400043638. 528pp.

In 1915, three cousins ruled great expanses of territory and huge populations of subjects—George, King of England; Nicholas, Tsar of Russia; and Wilhelm, Kaiser of Germany. Each man was positioned to bring their country into the 20th century, but "they were all three anachronisms, ill-equipped by education and personality to deal with the modern world, marooned by history in positions increasingly out of kilter with their era." This is the story of the historic shift from empire to democracy when the family alliances of hereditary rulers gave way to the power and will of the people. Carter tells the tale with clarity and insight into the psychology of each of these men, the complexity of their family interconnections, and the unfolding of 20th-century European history.

Darlow, Michael and Barbara Bray.
Ibn Saud: The Desert Warrior Who Created the Kingdom of Saudi Arabia. 2012. Skyhorse. 978-1616085797. 598pp.

British authors Darlow and Bray offer a fascinating look into the world of the Middle East, the family dynamics, and tribal politics that created a nation. Ibn Saud was a nomad and a warrior who through personal bravery, intelligence, and force of character founded the new Islamic state of Saudi Arabia in 1932. He oversaw the beginnings of the nation's rise in wealth from oil and guided Saudi Arabia through World War II as a neutral country though aligned with the Allies. This is an expansive book about one of history's men of destiny.

Hochschild, Adam. ♛
King Leopold's Ghost: A Story of Greed, Terror and Heroism in Colonial Africa. 1998. Houghton Mifflin. 978-0395759240. 384pp.

Leopold II (1835–1909) hated his Hapsburg wife, disdained his little country, and had no interest in his daughters after the death of his only son, but he was very interested in money and colonial expansion. Leopold—constitutional monarch of small, but increasingly democratic Belgium—became, through guile and terror, the totalitarian ruler of a vast African Empire where rubber and slave labor created wealth. The barbarous exploitation of the Congo was gradually revealed in Leopold's time by outraged observers and reverberated across Africa for years. This book, a best-selling prize winner that includes a large cast of colonial adventurers and whistle-blowers, is one of the best exemplars of history written as narrative storytelling.

Johnson, Paul.
Napoleon: A Life. 2002. Penguin. 978-0670030781. 208pp.

What made Napoleon who he was? He was a shrewd, decisive, driven leader who dominated the world scene for only about 15 years, yet he is one of the most studied and written about figures from history. This is a concise and insightful look at a complex life and an attempt to understand the phenomenon that was Napoleon. Johnson is a skillful writer, an unabashed conservative, and an unapologetically opinionated historian. This book is from the <u>Penguin Lives</u> series where prominent authors explore famous historical figures and do it in around 200 pages. Other books in the series include *Buddha* by Karen Armstrong, *Woodrow Wilson* by Louis Auchincloss, and *Branch Rickey* by Jimmy Breslin.

Massie, Robert K. ♛
Peter the Great: His Life and World. 1981. Random House (paperback). 978-0345298065. 928pp.

This Pulitzer Prize winner is an epic work about the dynamic tsar Peter (1672–1725) and his largely successful efforts to disengage Russia from its Eastern, medieval, and superstitious worldview and force it to embrace the modern scientific, economic, and cultural world of Europe and the West. Massie brilliantly explores the character of Peter, depicts his monumental undertakings, and places his portrait against the vast backdrop of Russia and Europe on the brink of modernity. Massie is also renowned for his other works about the Russian Romanov family *Nicholas and Alexandra* (1967) and his most recent Russian biography *Catherine the Great: Portrait of a Woman* (2011).

Penn, Thomas.
Winter King: Henry VII and the Dawn of Tudor England. 2012. Simon & Schuster. 978-1439191569. 480pp.

If Henry VIII was the Spring monarch and Elizabeth I the Summer monarch who each oversaw the flowering and fruition of Tudor England, then Henry VII, father and grandfather, was the Winter King who had made it all possible. Henry's claim to the throne was through maternal but bastard and therefore tenuous family lines. He seized the crown by battle in 1485, united the warring "Roses" of England by marrying Elizabeth of York, consolidated the crown's power through taxation and control of the nobility, instituted foreign policy aimed at peace, and created a court where conspiracy, spies, and paranoia played a large role, but he reigned for more than 20 years. Penn's book is a masterful look at Henry, his family, his court, and his country at the beginnings of Tudor England.

Wilson, Derek.
▶ *Charlemagne.* 2006. Doubleday. 0385516703. 226pp.

The son of a king, Charlemagne (742–814) was tall and imperial, a champion in war, a religious man, a believer in education, and a cunning administrator who understood power and the politics of his day. Charlemagne was a transformational leader. Wilson, a well-respected and prolific author of fiction and nonfiction, has written an intriguing and well-rounded life of the ruler who created Europe, defended Christendom, was a model for chivalry, and served as a (somewhat misinterpreted) role model for both Napoleon and Hitler. Justin Pollard's 2006 biography *Alfred the Great: The Man Who Made England* tells of another transformational early medieval king.

We Are Family—Family Sagas

Some families create history and their names populate history books (e.g., Borgia and Tudor, Adams and Kennedy, Rockefeller and Rothschild), while other families have just lived in history. If you like to read about a group of people linked together by blood and common interests, set against their historical, social, political, and economic milieu, then these are the books for you.

Aboulela, Leila.
Lyrics Alley. 2011. Grove. 0802119514. 304pp. FICTION

Aboulela offers a story that could be told of all families throughout history: the clash of tradition and modernity as younger family members face the future and older family members remember the past. Aboulela's story about the Abuzeid family living in 1950s Sudan and Cairo has a strong and evocative Middle Eastern setting redolent of coriander and mint, sunshine and paternalism, a waning British Empire, and an expanding sense of national and personal independence. Readers who want another family saga set in the context of Middle Eastern history should seek out Naguib Mahfouz's *Cairo Trilogy* beginning with *Palace Walk* (1988, originally published in Arabic in 1956).

Cote, Richard N.
Mary's World: Love, War, and Family Ties in Nineteenth-Century Charleston. 2000. Corinthian Books. 978-1929175048. 480pp.

This book could be classed as local history, but its story is not provincial. Mary Motte Alston Pringle (1803–1884) is central to this saga of an affluent family in Charleston, South Carolina—socially prominent, landholders, and slave owners—and their lives in the prosperous years before the Civil War and the turbulent years when war and the resultant social changes drastically altered their realities. Mary was a noble woman; her 13 children were interesting and varied. Using Mary's own letters and journals, Cote offers a glimpse into the American South and an extinct way of life.

de Waal, Edmund.

▶ *The Hare with Amber Eyes: A Hidden Inheritance.* 2010. Farrar, Straus, Giroux. 978-0374105976. 368pp.

De Waal looks at the effect of history on his large family, people he never knew, and who lived lives he can only vaguely reconstruct and imagine. His entry point to their story is the family's collection of 264 *netsuke*—small Japanese carvings made of ivory or wood, depicting little moments like a group of tortoises, a ripening fruit, a craftsman working on a barrel, etc. While his family—once fabulously wealthy Jewish bankers on a par with Rothschilds and Warburgs—suffered the 20th century's waves of persecution, dispersal, loss, and relocation, the little carvings endured and eventually became the possessions of the author. De Waal searches out his family's past and tells their story with poetry and profound emotion. This is a fascinating and unexpected look at history through the personal story of a family and a collection of art. *Good Living Street: Portrait of a Patron Family, Vienna 1900* (2011) by Tim Bonyhady tells the story of another 20th-century Viennese family.

Graham, Lawrence.

The Senator and the Socialite: The True Story of America's First Black Dynasty. 2006. HarperCollins. 978-0060184124. 455pp.

Blanche K. Bruce was the elected U.S. Senator from Mississippi who served from 1875 to 1881. His wife Josephine was a gracious and educated socialite whose father was a prominent dentist in Cleveland, Ohio. Together, they were a 19th-century Washington Power Couple. The unexpected part of their typical American success story is that they were both African Americans and Bruce had been born a slave; their lives followed a trajectory unusual for the time. For more stories of African American families, read *Slaves in the Family* (1998) by Edward Ball and *The Hairstons: An American Family in Black and White* (2000) by Henry Wiencek.

McKinney, Megan.

The Magnificent Medills: America's Royal Family of Journalism during a Century of Turbulent Splendor. 2011. Harper Collins. 978-0061782237. 448pp.

America's first media dynasty was the Medill family founded by Joseph Medill (an early supporter of Abraham Lincoln) and carried on by his children and grandchildren (who were Pattersons and McCormicks). In 1855, Joseph bought the *Chicago Tribune* and his descendants went on to publish the *New York Daily News*, the *Washington Times-Herald*, and *Newsday* all during the years when newspapers had readership and influence. McKinney presents several generations of history and gossip in this lively book about a colorful family of journalists, publishers, and socialites.

Rothschild, Emma.
The Inner Life of Empires: An Eighteenth Century History. 2011. Princeton. 978-0691148953. 496pp.

Rothschild presents the lives of the Johnstones, four sisters and seven brothers, born in Scotland in the 1720s and 1730s whose long and busy lives (the last sister didn't die until 1813) encompassed Revolution, Empire and Enlightenment. Their letters to each other used the language of Enlightenment ("public liberties" and "civil rights") to record the political changes they witnessed in Britain, the growth of the international commerce they prospered by, and to communicate their psychological lives back and forth. This is an unusually told story about a family of energetic and engaged people who lived privately during active, expansive years of the British Empire.

Waugh, Alexander.
House of Wittgenstein: A Family at War. 2009. Doubleday. 978-0385520607. 352pp.

Ludwig Wittgenstein was one of the premier philosophers of the 20th century, his brother Paul was a brilliant pianist who lost his right hand in World War I but continued his performing career perfecting complex one-handed pieces, two, perhaps three of their brothers committed suicide, their father was autocratic, their mother was introverted and nervous, and three sisters were equally peculiar, generally suffering from "tensions of a pathological and neurotic kind." This is the mesmerizing tale, set mainly in Vienna, London, and New York of a talented, eccentric, and tightly wound family with an excess of demons. Author Alexander Waugh himself comes from an illustrious and creative family that he wrote about in *Fathers and Sons: The Autobiography of a Family* (2004).

The Despicables—History's Bad Guys

From personal treachery and political betrayal to murder on a scale so massive it is unfathomable, these historical figures push the boundaries of what it means to be bad. In a list of history's unlovable men, you expect to see the 20th century's triumvirate of evil—Hitler, Stalin, and Mao—and newer works about these villains are included here. But also in this list are lesser bad guys who expressed evil in other ways: Thomas Cromwell, loyal and shrewd; Aaron Burr, brilliant and flawed; John Wilkes Booth, passionate and wrong; and J Bruce Ismay, selfish and misguided.

Chang, Jung and Jon Halliday.
Mao: The Unknown Story. 2005. Knopf. 0679422714. 814pp.

This riveting and detailed look at the life of one of the 20th century's biggest players has been criticized for being a biased polemic—a work that embellishes, exaggerates, and overly personalizes history. Perhaps, but authors Chang and Halliday argue that the facts of Mao are well known and not open to revisionism. Mao (1893–1976) was a driven and ruthless man and his story of grand-scale genocide and astonishingly petty vindictiveness makes for fascinating and sometimes repellant reading. The authors—husband and wife scholars—still hope to have the book published in Mainland China where they openly interviewed many survivors of Mao's era while researching this book.

Kershaw, Ian.
▶ *Hitler: A Biography.* 2008. Norton. 978-0393067576. 1,072pp.

Adolf Hitler was a "strange individual" and a "bizarre misfit." Despite inexperience, little education, and an unformed personality, Hitler willed himself to become the 20th century's—perhaps history's—most demonic leader. British historian and scholar Kershaw has written definitive volumes on Hitler, and this book is the abridged version of his authoritative two-volume work: *Hitler: 1889–1936 Hubris* (1999) and *Hitler: 1936–1945 Nemesis* (2000). Kershaw seeks to understand Hitler's power and to ascertain how Hitler was possible. Although this book is an abridgment, it is still a massive and comprehensive work that looks at the rise, impact, and downfall of Adolf Hitler.

Mantel, Hilary. ♛
Wolf Hall: A Novel. 2009. Henry Holt. 978-0805080681. 560pp. FICTION

Thomas Cromwell was Henry VIII's henchman. Cromwell (great-uncle to Oliver) was a Tudor personality to be reckoned with, a brilliant lawyer, a self-made man, student of Cardinal Wolsey, adviser to the Crown, and ultimately the fixer who took care of things when the king wanted a new wife. The 16th century is vividly portrayed in this novel of loyalty and perfidy. Mantel continues the story in *Bringing up the Bodies* (2012).

Montefiore, Simon Sebag.
Young Stalin. 2007. Knopf. 978-1400044658. 460pp.

Josef Djugashvili (1878–1953), a petty terrorist who learned politics from street fighting, changed his name to Stalin, which means steel, and came to lead one of the world's most populous countries with an almost unrivalled (see Mao) paranoid bloodlust. Historian Montefiore draws upon 10 years of research in 9 countries and 23 cities to write this comprehensive but intimate history of the man and his milieu. This book looks at the years prior to 1917 before Stalin had power, when he was a seminary student, husband to a doomed wife, bank robber, extortionist, arsonist, murderer, revolutionary, and budding political gangster who caught the eye of Lenin. Montefiore's earlier book *Stalin: The Court of the Red Tsar* (2004) details Stalin's later years in power.

Stewart, David O.
American Emperor: Aaron Burr's Challenge to Jefferson's America. 2011. Simon and Schuster. 978-1439157183. 432pp.

"A bright promise tarnished by treason, a traitor never punished, a terror never quite exorcised. Leading historian's wring their hands in dismay over Aaron Burr."—murderer, cheat, brilliant, ambitious, arrogant, a lady-killer, and an early feminist, in other words, a complex character. Stewart expands our understanding of Burr by looking at his scheme for America's western expansion and the trial that led Burr to escape to Europe for several years. For other looks at Aaron Burr, read Nancy Isenberg's *Fallen Founder: The Life of Aaron Burr* (2007), H. W. Brand's *The Heartbreak of Aaron Burr* (2012), or Gore Vidal's fictional account *Burr* (1973, reissued in 2000).

Swanson, James L.
Manhunt: The Twelve-Day Chase for Lincoln's Killer. 2006. William Morrow. 978-0060518493. 448pp.

The theatrical stage was too confining for John Wilkes Booth who wanted his actions to affect the world. He believed he would be lauded for avenging the defeat of the South by killing a tyrant, and on April 14, 1865, at Ford's Theater, he made his heroic stand and shot President Abraham Lincoln. The mindset of Booth, his vanity, amazing arrogance, and righteous belief in a defeated world are explored in this fast-paced retelling of the events surrounding the assassination of Lincoln and the escape and ultimate capture of Booth.

Wilson, Francis.
How to Survive the Titanic: Or the Sinking of J. Bruce Ismay. 2011. HarperCollins. 978-0062094544. 328pp.

When the White Star ship *Titanic* sank in April 1912, among the many famous and wealthy people on board was the managing director of the White Start Line, J. Bruce Ismay. When disaster struck, the order was given to save women and children, and men were turned back from the lifeboats, but J. Bruce Ismay took a place in a lifeboat. His actions on the ship and his answers at the subsequent hearings, in America and England, made him a hated man, reviled, despised, and considered cowardly and arrogant—he didn't have the fortitude to go down with the ship he owned. This is a compelling story of the final night on the great ship, the aftermath of the tragedy, and Ismay's privileged but strangely sad life.

Ordinary Folks, Extraordinary Stories

The simplicity of real lives against the backdrop of momentous historical moments makes for great reading. These are the stories of people you probably have never heard of, people caught up in the most epic moments in history—the Great Depression, Civil Rights, World War, and the Holocaust.

Dawson, George and Richard Glaubman.

▶ *Life Is So Good: One Man's Extraordinary Journey through the 20th Century and How He Learned to Read at Age 98.* 2001. Penguin (paperback). 0141001682. 260pp.

A life of hard work, socially sanctioned racism, and economic oppression never kept George Dawson from being a happy man. Born in Texas in 1898, the grandson of a slave, Dawson had to go to work instead of to school, but he lived the history of the 20th century and he recollects it all, as he says, "I've seen it all these hundred years, the good and the bad." Finally, after a life of work and raising family, he returned to school to learn to read. An upbeat story of a good man and a tumultuous century.

Gup, Ted.

A Secret Gift: How One Man's Kindness—and a Trove of Letters—Revealed the Hidden History of the Great Depression. 2010. Penguin. 1594202702. 368pp.

A family mystery in the form of a suitcase full of letters gives investigative journalist Gup a chance to use his professional skills on a personal mission. In 1933, the darkest days of the Great Depression, before FDR's New Deal kicked in, the residents of Canton, Ohio, are desperate for a little relief. Proud folk who wanted to work and were wary of charity answered a request placed in the Canton newspaper: "Tell me your story and I will send you some money." The seemingly inconsequential gift of a few dollars made a memorable difference to these people. Gup interviewed the children and grandchildren who remembered the Christmas that brought the gift and tells their story in this heartwarming tale about challenging times and human kindness.

Kalish, Mildred Armstrong.

Little Heathens: Hard Times and High Spirits on an Iowa Farm during the Great Depression. 2008. Bantam (paperback). 978-0553384246. 292pp.

Full of recipes, remedies, and reminiscences, this book was a surprise on multiple Best Book Lists for 2007. Kalish, an ex-English professor, tells her story of growing up on an Iowa farm during the Great Depression. It is a story full of joy, of happy memories, of hard work but no whining. She describes a "life of total involvement" where everyone in the multigenerational family did their share, pulled together, and had a good time doing it. Neither simpering nor sentimental, Kalish tells it like it was. She is an observant, cheerful, and warm-hearted author who makes splinters, outhouses, and even hog butchering sound almost fun.

Kirkpatrick, Jane.

The Daughter's Walk: A Novel. 2011. Waterbrook Press (paperback). 978-1400074297. 400pp. FICTION

True story: in 1896, indomitable Norwegian immigrant Helga Estby walked from Spokane, Washington, to New York City as a publicity stunt to promote women's suffrage and to advertise a more practical traveling skirt for women. Her goal was to earn prize money to pay off the mortgage of her family's farm. Her 19-year-old daughter walked with her. Kirkpatrick uses the story of the walk as a starting place to create the fictional story of the daughter who continued making her own way. A story of independence and personal growth expanded from a kernel of historical fact.

Kramer, Clara and Stephen Glantz.
Clara's War: One Girl's Story of Survival. 2009. Ecco. 978-0061728600. 368pp.

At the end of World War II, only 50 of the original 5,000 Jewish residents in the small Polish town of Zolkiew were alive. When the Russians liberated the town from the Nazis ragged, emaciated people climbed out of basements, down from attics, and came in from the woods and fields where they had hidden. Eighteen people emerged from under a house where for 18 months they had lived in dirt eating little more than potatoes. Teenager Clara Schwarz and several of her family survive this great nightmare, thanks to the anti-Semitic, arrogant, hard drinking, adulterous, German gentile Valentine Beck, who hides them, provides for them, blusters to protect them, and makes himself responsible for their lives. A powerful Holocaust story about a family swept up in history and an unlikely hero.

Nez, Chester and Judith Scheiss Avila.
Code Talker: The First and Only Memoir by One of the Original Navajo Code Talkers of WWII. 2011. Berkley/Penguin. 978-0425244234. 310pp.

Nez's firsthand World War II narrative is fast paced and thrilling. Nez tells of growing up fully enveloped in Navajo culture, attending government-run boarding schools in the 1920s where he was punished for speaking his native language, then enlisting in the Marines shortly after Pearl Harbor, and using the previously forbidden language to develop a code that baffled the Japanese and helped American forces win previously unattainable victories in the Pacific theater. The pastoral, placid, and very poor traditional life of his father and grandparents was a sharp contrast to the beach landings, battle scenes, and foxhole life on the islands of Guadalcanal, Guam, and Bougainville. Instrumental in the Pacific victories, Nez and his fellow code talkers were forbidden to discuss their contributions to the war until their mission was declassified in 1968. In telling his story, Nez displays the bravery, honor, and stoicism of his native Navajo culture and his marine training.

Salisbury, Gay and Laney Salisbury.
The Cruelest Miles: The Heroic Story of Dogs and Men in a Race against an Epidemic. 2003. Norton. 978-0393019629. 317pp.

Nome, Alaska, one of America's most isolated cities, is icebound for seven months of the year. In the 1920s, it had a small, vibrant urban society and a surrounding community sparsely populated with native peoples and civilization's loners. But Nome was not immune to disaster, and in 1925, diphtheria struck and within a few weeks, several children were dead and the town was quarantined.

The only solution was a large quantity of the diphtheria antitoxin readily available but thousands of miles away. The world, kept informed by telegrams, waited in suspense to see if dogsleds led by Togo, Balto, the other heroic dogs, and the 20 men who drove them would survive the frigid nonstop 674-mile journey from the nearest rail station to fetch the lifesaving antitoxin and rescue the children of Nome. This is an inherently exciting story about the heroism of regular folks and the nobility of the intrepid dogs told by the Salisburys with great energy and deep reverence for the past.

Skloot, Rebecca.
The Immortal Life of Henrietta Lacks. 2010. Crown. 978-1400052172. 384pp.
   Though her life was brief, Henrietta Lacks has served humanity beyond her actual death because cells from her body, taken without her knowledge when she was a cancer patient at Johns Hopkins in 1951, have never died. Those cells—known to the scientific and medical communities as HeLa cells—have endlessly replicated, been packaged and sold, and been the basis of numberless trials and experiments contributing to the polio vaccine and DNA research. This is the personal story of her life, the lives of her children and family who only gradually came to know the truth, and the scientists, doctors, and lab technicians who worked with her cells. Skloot does an excellent mash-up of science, humanity, and ethics in this dynamic story.

Turner, Steve.
The Band that Played On: The Extraordinary Story of the 8 Musicians Who Went Down with the Titanic. 2011. Thomas Nelson. 978-1595552198. 272pp.
   Live musical entertainment was a standard offering on cruise ships in the early 1900s, and eight men were on board the *Titanic* to play music at afternoon tea, lunch, and dinner to create a mood of sophistication and serenity. The musicians on the *Titanic* in April 1912 were virtual strangers to one another, three had not even been to sea before, but each was talented and well trained, and all had chosen an adventurous venue. On the night the ship sank, the musicians on the *Titanic* gathered on deck with their instruments and played music to calm the passengers. All the musicians perished. Each was eulogized as a model of courage, fortitude, and self-sacrifice. The dramas on the *Titanic* continue to mesmerize us 100 years after the disaster. This book offers another look at the multifaceted story by searching out the backgrounds and sacrificed futures of eight of the men who died that night.

Creative Spirits and Their Times

The artist has always had a special place in the story. Slightly outside the mainstream of politics and economics, artists take moments of our lives and reflect them back to us adding depth to the human experience. This mix of artists' lives offers a look at how the creative spirit has both reflected and created history.

Bentley, Toni.
Sisters of Salome. 2002. Yale. 0300090390. 223pp.

The question posed by author Toni Bentley in this book is "Why did these women dance naked?" Through daring acts of self-creation, four women used the mythic framework of the biblical Salome, dancer, seductress, and femme fatale to express their own feminine reality. Bentley, a former Balanchine ballerina, explores the lives and creative worlds of Mata Hari, performer and spy; the author Colette; and dancers Ida Rubinstein and Maud Allen in an attempt to understand the enduring power of the figure of Salome, the need of the public to gaze at women, and the desire of these women to create art at the edge of social acceptability.

Egan, Timothy.
Short Nights of the Shadow Catcher: The Epic Life and Immortal Photographs of Edward Curtis. 2012. Houghton Mifflin Harcourt. 978-0618969029. 370pp.

Edward Curtis was a studio photographer in Seattle on the cusp of the 20th century. But he found a calling and a passion outside of the studio, photographing Native Americans—famous chiefs and anonymous subjects—all depicting the vanishing native cultures of America. Curtis evolved from just photographing his subjects to conducting an almost full-scale anthropological study making recordings of Indian language, music, and lore and compiling his work in 20 volumes funded by J. P. Morgan and with a foreword by Theodore Roosevelt. Curtis struggled with money, family, his patron, and even his own motivation, yet he left behind a massive amount of material documenting an America that no longer exists.

Gabler, Neal.
▶ *Walt Disney: The Triumph of the American Imagination.* 2006. Knopf. 978-0679438229. 880pp.

This massive biography tells the story of Walt Disney and the creation of an empire. Disney's personal life, creative advances, and business dealings are detailed. Though he grew up with a rather joyless father, Disney himself was an optimist and a perfectionist and was overflowing with entrepreneurial courage. He had a lifelong ally in his stalwart brother, Roy Disney, who was crucial to the business success of their company; and Disney himself was a true genius, a master storyteller, and an innovator bringing sound, color, and on-screen personality to animation. A good companion to this work is *Building a Company: Roy O Disney and the Creation of an Entertainment Empire* (1998) by Bob Thomas.

Gaines, James R.
Evening in the Palace of Reason: Bach Meets Frederick the Great in the Age of Enlightenment. 2005. Harper. 978-0007156580. 352pp.

In this dual biography, Gaines looks at Johann Sebastian Bach (1685–1750), the brilliant composer whose music continues to challenge and edify listeners, and Frederick II of Prussia (1712–1786), who became known as Frederick the Great, military genius, domestic reformer, patron of the arts, and remembered in history as being monumentally abused by his own mad father. Bach and Frederick met in 1747 when Frederick summoned Bach to his court. Gaines uses this meeting as an opening to explore the lives of these two men and their influence on art, politics, and the European world during the blossoming of the Enlightenment when reason superseded faith as the guiding principle of musicians and kings. *The Ninth: Beethoven and the World in 1824* (2010) by Harvey Sachs is another recommended story of musical genius.

Holroyd, Michael.
A Strange Eventful History: The Dramatic Lives of Ellen Terry, Henry Irving, and Their Remarkable Families. 2009. FSG. 978-0374270803. 620pp.

Ellen Terry lived a big life. She was a Victorian era superstar, the premier English stage actress of her time, and a luminescent personality who "felt everything very deeply but nothing for long." Her frequent costar was Henry Irving, another larger-than-life Victorian superstar who was Terry's opposite and complement in every way. Their creative lives and the lives of their husbands, wives, lovers, and children form the world of this book. Terry's son Gordon Craig—actor, director, artistic designer, and expansive creative character in his own right—as well as Lewis Carroll, George Bernard Shaw, Isadora Duncan, Bram Stoker, Alfred Tennyson, and Vita Sackville-West are just a few players with walk-on roles in this look at two of the English theater's most accomplished families.

Hyland, William.
Gershwin: A New Biography. 2003. Praeger. 0275981118. 279pp.

Can you hear the strains of *Rhapsody in Blue, An American in Paris, Porgy and Bess, Swanee, Someone to Watch over Me*? All music composed by George Gershwin who helped to create the soundtrack for 20th-century America. Born in New York in 1898, the son of Russian Jewish immigrants, Gershwin seemed always to be in the right place at the right time with the right talent—in Tin Pan Alley when the American Songbook was being created, on Broadway when operettas and reviews were morphing into musical comedy, and in Hollywood when the big screen musical was poised to flourish. This insightful, balanced biography gives a good understanding of the man, his talent, and his times. Interesting read-arounds to this book are *The Memory of All That: George Gershwin, Kay Swift, and My Families' Legacy of Infidelities* (2011) by Katherine Weber and *The House that George Built: With a Little Help from Irving, Cole and a Crew of about Fifty* (2007) by Wilfred Sheed about the rise of the popular song.

Martin, Justin.
Genius of Place: The Life of Frederick Law Olmsted. 2011. Da Capo. 978-0306818813. 496pp.

Frederick Law Olmsted did many things during his long life (1822–1903) and he did all of them well, but he is primarily known as America's first landscape architect famous for designing Central Park, the U.S. Capitol grounds, and the extensive grounds of the Biltmore Estate in North Carolina. But more than a landscape designer, Olmsted was a humane and empathetic man who served during the Civil War as head of the U.S. Sanitary Commission (precursor to the Red Cross) where he organized hospital ships. During his career he also designed grounds for several mental institutions aiming to create an environment to calm shattered souls. This is a highly readable story of America in the 19th century and the biography of a creative, artistic yet practical man who redesigned our experience of the outdoors and brought nature back into the urban experience

Rhodes, Richard.
Hedy's Folly: The Life and Breakthrough Inventions of Hedy Lamarr, the Most Beautiful Woman in the World. 2011. Doubleday. 978-0385534383. 261pp.

Actress and renowned beauty Hedy Lamarr liked to spend her free time inventing things. Together with avant-garde composer George Antheil, she created a jam proof radio system for guiding torpedoes that used frequency hopping to rapidly change channels. They were granted a patent in 1942. Their concept was later known as spread-spectrum technology and was one of the foundations for cell phones and wireless networks. Rhodes tells the story of how this Viennese teenager who talked her way into the movies and became a star and a composer who once lived above the Shakespeare and Company bookstore in Paris met in Hollywood and tinkered together an invention they hoped would beat the Nazis and win the war.

Vreeland, Susan.
The Passion of Artemisia: A Novel. 2002. Viking. 0670894494. 288pp. FICTION

Artemisia Gentileschi was a painter who captured the drama of life through vibrant colors on bold canvases in 17th-century Italy. Though she has come down through time as one of the greatest female painters, her life was often filled with hardship and humiliation. Vreeland offers the story of a brilliant artist's life lived boldly in a time hostile to women with talent. Follow up with Vreeland's other works about the lives of artists, *The Forest Lover* (2004) about painter Emily Carr and *Luncheon of the Boating Party* (2007) about Paris and the Impressionists.

Well-Behaved Women Seldom Make History

> Well-behaved women seldom make history.
> —Laurel Thatcher Ulrich

Amanda Foreman's best seller *Georgianna: Duchess of Devonshire* (2001) exposed 18th-century British power politics and aristocratic shenanigans through the life of one enthralling woman. Since its success, readers have sought out biographies of singular women in the context of their times. And scholars have obliged with these traditional biographies about untraditional women.

Cordery, Stacy A.
Alice: Alice Roosevelt Longworth, from White House Princess to Washington Power Broker. 2007. Penguin. 978-0670018338. 608pp.

Alice Roosevelt, President Theodore Roosevelt's eldest daughter, was America's First Teenager, a lively, rebellious girl who smoked on the White House roof and wrote in her diary about boys she liked, who grew into a strong woman, a politically astute Washington personality, and an unconventional character who didn't seek office, but still lived in the public eye. Intelligent, witty, and outspoken Princess Alice loved politics and the spotlight. The story of her long life (1884–1980) is recounted with depth and psychological acuity in this volume by Cordery, who is also the author of *Juliette Gordon Low: The Remarkable Founder of the Girl Scouts* (2012).

Duffy, Stella.
Theodora: Actress, Empress, Whore. 2010. Virago. 978-1844082155. FICTION

Like all great characters, Theodora contained multitudes—she was pious and lusty, beautiful and shrewish, yearning to be cared for but needing to make her own way. The daughter of a bear trainer who died when she was a young girl, Theodora and her sisters earned their livings as performers. Theodora became a trained actress, a successful whore, and around AD 525, Empress of the Byzantine Empire when she married the Emperor Justinian I. She was an early feminist championing equal social and economic rights for women, an able consort who helped her husband rule wisely, and ultimately she was made a saint in the Greek Orthodox Church. Set in the exotic Byzantine world, Duffy's sexy novel presents a possible version of Theodora's life.

Gorn, Elliott.
Mother Jones: The Most Dangerous Woman in America. 2002. Hill and Wang. 978-0809070947. 432pp.

Born in Ireland in 1837, Marry Harris survived the Irish potato famine and a harsh immigration to Canada with her family. As a young mother, she survived the Memphis Yellow Fever epidemic that swept away her husband and four little children. In 1871, she survived the Great Chicago Fire. Not until she was well into her 60s did she become Mother Jones, a galvanizing leader and an icon to workers who fought to expose the abuses of management and inspire America's laborers to unite and fight. Although she published her own autobiography in 1925, it is recognized as incomplete and often inaccurate—she crafted a story she wanted told. Gorn's book adds back the remarkable truth of this woman who fought "like hell for the living."

Howell, Georgina.
Gertrude Bell: Queen of the Desert, Shaper of Nations. 2007. Farrar, Straus and Giroux. 978-0374161620. 512pp.

Spirited, self-confident, and possessor of an outstanding intellect and boundless energy, Bell was a driving force in the early 20th-century establishment of Iraq and the modern Arab world. A happy Victorian childhood, a rare university education, but little luck in love led Bell to travel and become an expert on the Middle East, its archaeology, poetry, language, and people. Her life was surprisingly full of adventure and she undertook it all with archetypal British *sangfroid*. Solid research, brisk writing, and a spirited subject make this a great read. To learn about a kindred spirit (who hated being compared to Bell), read *Passionate Nomad: The Life of Freya Stark* (1999) by Jane Fletcher Geniesse.

Pakula, Hannah.
The Last Empress: Madame Chiang Kai-Shek and the Birth of Modern China. 2009. Simon & Schuster. 1439148937. 816pp.

Beautiful and alluring, charming and capable, Madame Chiang Kai-Shek was born into the wealthy and prominent Soong family in Shanghai in 1898. As May-ling Soong, she attended Wellesley College in the United States and graduated with a degree in English. She went on to become the First Lady of the Republic of China as the wife of Chinese leader, the Generalissimo, Chiang Kai-Shek. Her story is the story of China in the 20th century, a tumultuous and complex history of politics, revolution, and international maneuvering. Madame was a strong, talented, and intelligent woman who kept China in the Western news from the 1930s on. She died in 2003 in New York City at the age of 105. Pakula's book is comprehensive and substantial yet reads like an epic family saga.

Shipman, Pat.
▶ *Femme Fatale: Love, Lies, and the Unknown Life of Mata Hari.* 2007. William Morrow. 978-0060817282. 464pp.

Executed war criminal, inept spy, sensual performer, abused wife, abandoned child—Mata Hari played many roles. In the early 1900s, Margaretha Zelle MacLeod, a woman who loved luxury and whose main talents were sensuous movement and serious flirtation, made herself into the exotic dancer Mata Hari so she could get what she wanted out of life. But her trusting naïveté ultimately led her to a place in front of a French firing squad, convicted of being a German spy in the midst of World War I. Shipman sympathetically explores the life of a woman who was condemned "not for espionage, but for her lack of shame."

Animals and Their People

The interplay of humans and animals has always been part of the bigger story of history—animals scare us, work for us, amuse us, love us, and are loved by us; and memorable animal protagonists like Seabiscuit, the racehorse, and

Dewey, the library cat, have enthralled us. Stories of the interactions between people and animals across time and cultures will always have appeal.

Allin, Michael.
Zarafa: A Giraffe's True Story, from Deep in Africa to the Heart of Paris. 1998. Walker. 978-0802713391. 224pp.

In 1826, Muhammad Ali, ruler of Egypt, sent a gift to Charles X, King of France—a young giraffe. Journey with Zarafa down the Nile, across the Mediterranean, and then from Marseille to Paris, walking the entire way by "small, daily journeys" over the course of a summer. She remained in Paris for 18 years, an exotic yet gentle delight to citizens and visitors. This is a small book as elegant as the animal character it portrays, but it touches on a wide canvas—Napoleon's time in Egypt and his *corps des savants* there, the beginnings of Egyptology as a discipline, Champollion and the Rosetta stone, Marie Therese and Charles X of France, and the introduction of exotic animals to civilized Parisian society.

Belozerskaya, Marina.
The Medici Giraffe: And Other Tales of Exotic Animals and Power. 2006. Little, Brown. 978-0316525657. 432pp.

The intersection of exotic animals and human society is a recurring theme across history. Though familiar to us now, wild and exotic animals once filled humanity with terror and awe. In beautiful prose, Belozerskaya tells the stories of Pompey's animal-gladiatorial games, Montezuma's zoo, and William Randolph Hearst's private menagerie at San Simeon. She narrates how the symbolic power of wild and rare animals led the Renaissance Medici to use lions and giraffes to display their strength and 20th-century Chinese officials to give pandas to the United States as gestures of friendship and détente. As much about humans and their times as the animals, this is an informative and elegant collection of essays that asks readers to think about man's historic and psychological relation to beast.

Chambers, Paul.
Jumbo: This Being the True Story of the Greatest Elephant in the World. 2008. Steerforth Press. 978-1586421410. 232pp.

Everyone thinks their elephant is the greatest, but Jumbo really was the greatest and one of the first to be known to the world at large. Captured in Africa in 1862, Jumbo lived for years in the Victorian era at the London Zoo tended by his faithful keeper Matthew Scott. Sold to showman P. T. Barnum in 1880, Jumbo ended his years as a circus attraction in America where his size and personality made him a beloved star. In the tradition of all great animal stories, Jumbo's finale will break your heart.

Coren, Stanley.
The Pawprints of History: Dogs and the Course of Human Events. 2002. Free Press. 978-0743222280. 322pp.

The dog has been man's best friend for 15,000 years. Though the contributions of dogs as hunters, herders, explorers, and warriors have been recorded, the impact of dogs on the liberal arts, creative realms, politics, and psychology is less well known. Scholar and author Stanley Coren corrects that oversight by presenting stories of famous people and the dogs they loved. In his uplifting book, Coren shows dogs as the companions, protectors, creative inspirations, and loyal friends of such diverse people as Sigmund Freud, Richard Wagner, Walter Scott, Frederick the Great, and several American presidents. Combining his interests in history, biography, psychology, and dogs, Coren, a professor of psychology, illuminates the hidden pawprints of history in this easy-reading compendium.

Morpurgo, Michael.
War Horse. 2007 (originally published in 1982). Scholastic. 978-0439796637. 165pp. FICTION Ⓨ Ⓐ

Experience the mud, violence, and terror of the World War I as narrated by a horse who served on the front line. This spare, lovely story about the horrors of war and the endurance of love will remind readers of *Black Beauty* by Anna Sewell and *Bel Ria: Dog of War* by Sheila Burnford.

Orlean, Susan.
▶ *Rin Tin Tin: The Life and the Legend.* 2011. Simon and Schuster. 978-1439190135. 336pp.

Rin Tin Tin's story is a very American rags-to-riches-to-rags tale. Lee Duncan, an American serving in France in 1918, discovered a litter of newborn German Shepherd pups cowering with their frantic mother amongst the corpses of other dogs in a bombed-out battlefield kennel. Duncan takes one of the pups to California where he lovingly trains the dog, and together they look for work in the movies. The rest, as they say, is history. Rin Tin Tin goes on to become a media sensation, a standout animal star in silent movies, and later a hero on television. Orlean's story is about an individual dog and his descendants, the creation and expansion of the German Shepherd breed, the vagaries and ultimate cruelties of Hollywood, and the lives of two ordinary men who made and lost fortunes controlling the image of a dog that was better, braver, and nobler than all the rest. Orlean writes flowing, conversational prose and brings great empathy to her topic.

Rivas, Mim Eichler.
Beautiful Jim Key: The Lost History of a Horse and a Man Who Changed the World. 2005. William Morrow. 978-0060567033. 352pp.

Before Man-of-War, Seabiscuit, or Mr. Ed, there was Beautiful Jim Key (1889–1912)—the amazing horse who could spell, do arithmetic, flirt, debate politics, and seemingly think independently. His trainer and owner, Dr. William Key—an ex-slave, a veteran of the Civil War, and a self-taught doctor of veterinary medicine—had a talent with animals. Using patience and kindness, Dr. Key trained the special horse to be a performer who delighted and amazed audiences around America. At one time, Big Jim's box-office take was bigger than either John Phillip Sousa's or Sarah Bernhardt's and the attention he gained created new respect for the humane treatment of animals. Rivas writes a great story about the most famous horse you never heard of, a horse with the talent and charisma of a superstar.

It's Not Easy Being Queen—The (Mostly Sad) Lives of Princesses and Queens

It sounds so lovely to be a princess. Always wearing pink, forever eating cupcakes, singing duets with birds, but wait, that is a four-year-old girl's idea of how a princess lives. Throughout history, the reality of being royal was very different and for many, being a princess or queen meant a life of danger, dismissal, or doom.

Buckley, Veronica.
Christina, Queen of Sweden: The Restless Life of a European Eccentric. 2004. Harper. 978-0060736170. 384pp.

One of history's most interesting characters—a queen who gave up her throne and forsook her country in search of personal freedom, a woman who dressed and often behaved like a man, yet acted like a queen no matter where she found herself—Christina was eccentric, restless, willful, dynamic, and intelligent. Taking the throne on the death of her father when she was a six-year-old girl, Christina was Queen of Sweden for 21 years until she voluntarily abdicated in 1654. Determined to be free of the obligation to rule and rid of the cold and censure of Sweden, she moved to Rome, became a Catholic, and lived a life of unrepentant scandal until her death in 1689. More scholarly than sensational, this is an insightful read about one of history's unconventional queens.

Fox, Julia.
Sister Queens: The Noble, Tragic Lives of Katherine of Aragon and Juana, Queen of Castile. 2012. Ballantine. 978-0345516046. 480pp.

Katherine and Juana, daughters of Queen Isabel and King Ferdinand of Spain, were each sent from home, family, and country as teenagers, destined to be the brides of kings. Katherine went to England to marry Arthur, heir to King Henry VII and, when Arthur died leaving her a young widow, to languish in England until his brother, Henry VIII, took her as his own bride and queen. Juana married Phillip of Burgundy, and a marriage designed to consolidate territory became a true love match that resulted in six children. Upon Phillip's death in 1506, when Juana tried to assert her right to rule what is now modern Spain, she was imprisoned by her father and eventually her son, deemed mad, and referred to ever after as *Juana la Loca*. Fox creates a vivid portrait of the world of these 16th-century queens who were married and then marginalized, each powerful, educated, and intelligent yet neither in control of her own fate.

Fraser, Flora.
▶ *Princesses: The Six Daughters of George III.* 2005. Knopf. 978-0679451181. 496pp.

While King George III of England was fighting the American colonists and later facing a bout of madness, his daughters were living a soap opera of their own. Their mother Queen Charlotte, a woman of strong personality, bore 15 children and raised them all with care and attention and her daughters became accomplished, well-educated women who were stultified by family duty and loyalty. Raised to be consorts to kings, they were forbidden by their parents to leave home and pursue their own lives. Fraser tells all in this book about the lives of six forgotten English princesses.

Gelardi, Julia.
From Splendor to Revolution: The Romanov Women, 1847–1928. 2011. St. Martin's Press. 978-0312371159. 482pp.

Gelardi tells the intertwining stories of four imperial women—an empress, a queen, a duchess, and a grand duchess—each by birth or marriage a member of Russian royalty. All were wives and mothers, all were participants in the opulence and excess of Imperial Russia, and each lived through the maelstrom of Revolution that destroyed their fortunes, their ideals, and their families. Their love stories, liaisons, and family dramas are played out against tumultuous European politics and history from 1847 to 1928. Gelardi, who has also written about Queen Victoria's daughters, offers an engrossing read with a cast so large that her book includes four family trees and a seven page list of *dramatis personae*.

Min, Anchee.
Empress Orchid. 2004. Mariner (paperback). 0618562036. 368pp. FICTION.

The early years of China's last empress come alive in this detailed novel about the exotic, complex, and stifling life of the Chinese imperial court. In the last half of the 1800s as China is being forced to open herself to the Western world, 17-year-old Orchid is living with her family in deepening poverty when she learns she is eligible to become a concubine to the emperor. After a crash course in court etiquette, Orchid makes the attempt and is chosen! But her travails have just begun as she enters the Forbidden City and the treacherous world of concubines, eunuchs, and political and sexual rivals. Although Orchid's intelligence and strong spirit take her to the top, history is unclear about her character: Was she a shrewd politician who helped China during her lifetime or a scheming woman who became a scapegoat to history? To see how the story continues, read Anchee Min's follow up, *The Last Empress* (2007).

Nagel, Susan.
Marie-Therese: The Fate of Marie Antoinette's Daughter. 2008. Bloomsbury. 978-1596910577. 418pp.

The precious daughter of Louis XVI and Marie Antoinette spent four years of her adolescence as a prisoner of the revolution—separated from her family and given no information about their fates. She refused to speak to her captors, and consequently spoke to no one for years. When finally released, she endured perpetual exile from the country she should have ruled. Nagel depicts the excess of royal life before the revolution, the turbulence and terror of the revolution, and the wanderings of a woman of regal demeanor, courage, and dignity, who forgave the murderers of her family and maintained an enduring loyalty to France. Follow up with one of the recent compelling books about Marie-Therese's famous mother, Marie Antoinette, like Caroline Weber's *Queen of Fashion: What Marie Antoinette Wore to the Revolution* (2006) or Sena Jeter Naslund's *Abundance: A Novel of Marie Antoinette* (2006).

Schiff, Stacy. 🏆
Cleopatra: A Life. 2010. Little Brown and Company. 978-0316001922. 368pp.

Schiff does a masterful job of removing the mystery from Cleopatra and presenting the rich, full life of a beautiful woman who ruled her country with intelligence and cunning. Femme fatale, power broker, politician, diplomat, goddess, and queen, Cleopatra was undoubtedly the most powerful woman of her time, and she did what needed to be done to protect her nation, her children, and herself. A great read about another doomed queen who nevertheless put up a good fight.

Siler, Julia Flynn.
Lost Kingdom: Hawaii's Last Queen, the Sugar Kings and America's First Imperial Adventure. 2012. Atlantic Monthly. 978-0802120014. 480pp.

The Kingdom of Hawaii had a long royal history prior to its encounters with the rest of the world. The last queen, Lili'uokalani, was forced to abdicate because the riches of Hawaii—mainly sugar—and Hawaii's strategic position in the Pacific Ocean were coveted by more powerful forces, like England, France, and the ultimate victor, the United States. Lili'uokalani was a contemporary of Queen Victoria, a champion for the rights of her people—the dwindling population of native Hawaiians. She was a poet and a gracious lady whose right to rule was set aside so outsiders could profit from her abundant homeland. A dramatic story of imperialism, greed, and the grace of a true queen.

Brainiacs—Big Minds Thinking Great Thoughts

The big brains of the past always fascinate. How are they able to see the world so differently from the rest of us and to use their big brains and unique visions to advance us all? Characters of genius are explored in these books.

Feldman, Burton and Katherine Williams.
▶ *112 Mercer Street: Einstein, Russell, Gödel, Pauli, and the End of Innocence in Science.* 2007. Arcade. 978-1559707046. 242pp.

In the winter of 1943–1944, at Albert Einstein's house in Princeton, while World War II was being fought around the globe and the atomic bomb was being developed at Los Alamos, four of the world's great brains met once a week to talk. Albert Einstein, Bertrand Russell, Kurt Gödl, and Wolfgang Pauli left no record of what they discussed, but Burton uses the fact of the weekly gatherings to look at the lives of these geniuses and their contributions to science, specifically mathematics and physics. Surrounding them in the New Jersey winter were the spirits and ideas of other great thinkers they had known, studied under, worked with, argued with, and influenced—Heisenberg, Mach, Bohr, Oppenheimer, and others. This is a lively, brief first step into the world of quantum physics.

Gertner, Jon.
The Idea Factory: The Bell Labs and the Great Age of American Innovation. 2012. Penguin. 978-1594203282. 422pp.

Silicon Valley was born in New Jersey and the components of modern communication—transistors, satellites, fiber optics, and semiconductors— were developed by a group of eccentric and brilliant men at the Bell Labs from 1920 to 1980. A scientific enterprise as well as a commercial concern, Bell Labs were established by AT&T to support the telephone monopoly, but the synergy of the intellects employed by the lab created the future. A seemingly dry and potentially intimidating subject is made personable and intriguing by Gertner's observations of the men involved and his friendly, sometimes humorous prose, at Bell Labs he notes, "Experiments sometimes literally exploded." For more 20th-century big brains, read *Turing's Cathedral: The Origins of the Digital Age* (2012) by George Dyson and *The Information: A History, a Theory, a Flood* (2011) by James Gleick.

Heilbroner, Robert L.
The Worldly Philosophers: The Lives, Times and Ideas of the Great Economic Thinkers. 1999 (seventh edition, originally published in 1953). Touchstone (paperback). 978-0684862149. 368pp.

This classic book looks at the lives and theories of the men who thought deeply about the economic reality of human existence, wrote their theories down, and thereby affected history not through military might, politics, or personal magnetism, but by their ideas. Heilbroner looks at Adam Smith, Maynard Keynes, and Joseph Schumpeter with discussion of Marx, Malthus, and others along the way. A seminal work that offers a foundation for economic thinking and understanding.

King, David.
Finding Atlantis: A True Story of Genius, Madness, and an Extraordinary Quest for a Lost World. 2005. Harmony. 1400047528. 320pp.

Olof Rudbeck—Swedish academic professor of medicine, botanist, anatomist, astronomer, and scholar of ancient Viking sagas—strode the world's intellectual stage after Galileo but before Newton. Rudbeck had a large personality, an expansive mind, and a thrilling story that is little known today perhaps because his *magnum opus*, a scholarly tome called *Atlantica*, attempted to prove that the fabled land of Atlantis was actually Sweden—a misguided mission, perhaps, but his scholarship was impeccable. King vibrantly depicts the European scene of the time and writes with swift pacing about an engaging main character and a little-known corner of intellectual history.

Pearl, Daniel.

The Technologists: A Novel. 2012. Random House. 978-1400066575. 496pp. FICTION

A new school of technology is struggling to establish itself, but it is viewed with suspicion by the people, attacked by the press, and derided by the students at well-established Harvard. But when a series of unexplainable violent events wracks the venerable city of Boston, can the "technologists" of the new MIT, 19th-century nerds, help solve the crimes? Pearl offers a mix of history and fiction in this entertaining novel that forces readers to ponder the power of technology, the expansion of knowledge, and the true value of progress. Also seek out Pearl's 2003 best seller *The Dante Club* in which Oliver Wendell Holmes, James Russell Lowell, and Henry Wadsworth Longfellow work together to solve a mystery.

Snyder, Laura J.

The Philosophical Breakfast Club: Four Remarkable Friends Who Transformed Science and Changed the World. 2011. Broadway Books. 978-0307716170. 439pp.

Charles Babbage, inventor of the first computer; Richard Jones, political economist; John Herschel, astronomer and early photographer; and William Whewell, theologian and historian who coined the word "scientist," were friends who explored the ideas of science together for almost 60 years from their early days as Cambridge students to the death of the last man in 1871. These were men who believed in the creativity and artistry of science but were also polymaths who contributed to the codification of science as a field of study with methods, rules, expectations of accuracy, and academic rigor. The intellectual scope of Snyder's book is immense, and yet it is a chatty and approachable read about Victorian England, the history of science, and four interesting men.

Sobel, Dava.

A More Perfect Heaven: How Copernicus Revolutionized the Cosmos. 2011. Walker & Company. 978-0802717931. 288pp.

In a time of religious, political, and social upheaval, a scientific revolution was also fomenting. Copernicus (1473–1543), working quietly in a sleepy corner of Poland, could now prove a fact that would upset the world—the Earth revolved around the Sun. His journey to this knowledge and his 30-year internal struggle over how to tell the world form the basis of this new work by renowned science historian Dava Sobel. Sobel is an accomplished writer who takes complex historical moments and scientific discoveries and transforms them into compelling reading.

Wulf, Andrea.
The Brother Gardeners: Botany, Empire and the Birth of an Obsession. 2008. Knopf. 978-0307270238. 354pp.
　　The pleasures of gardening and the science of botany were revolutionized in 18th-century England by three Englishmen, an American, and two Swedes according to Wulf's clever exploration of horticultural history. Major figures like Benjamin Franklin, Captain Bligh, and Captain Cook become walk-ons in this delightfully original history that tells the story of friendships and empires forged through the discovery, acquisition, and love of plants and flowers. Wulf covers similar territory in *Founding Gardeners: The Revolutionary Generation, Nature, and the Shaping of the American Nation* (2011).

Passionate Connections—History's Famous Couples

Can historians ever truly understand the private life of a man and a woman? Closed doors don't stop speculation and we still want to know what is happening though the pen has been put down and the cameras have stopped recording. These books look at couples whose names still ring across the years as a man and a woman who were passionately connected.

Brady, Patricia.
A Being So Gentle: The Frontier Love Story of Rachel and Andrew Jackson. 2011. Palgrave. 978-0230609501. 272pp.
　　In 1785, Rachel Donelson married Lewis Robards, then in 1789, Rachel Robards eloped with Andrew Jackson. Uncertainty over the date of her divorce from her first husband followed this new couple for years and became a recurring issue and scandal fodder in the public life of Andrew Jackson, the future president of the United States. But the relationship of Rachel and Andrew was a true love match that withstood any gossip and they lived together for almost 40 years devoted to each other the entire time. This brisk biography tells the love story of Rachel and Andrew Jackson set in the context of the Westward expansion of America. For the story of another American couple who helped create the nation, try *Passion and Principle: John and Jessie Fremont, the Couple Whose Power, Politics, and Love Shaped Nineteenth-Century America* (2007) by Sally Denton.

Burge, James.
Heloise & Abelard: A New Biography. 2003. Harper Collins. 0060736631. 319pp.
　　Young, lovely, bright Heloise was to be educated by the famous clergyman and teacher Peter Abelard. Older, intelligent, and presumably more worldly

wise than the virginal Heloise, Abelard was nevertheless smitten with his lively protégé, and the two began an illicit affair. Scholar Burge uses a trove of newly discovered letters attributed to the pair to explore the relationship of these famous medieval lovers whose burning passion and story of tragedy and separation transcends the centuries and continues to appeal to romantics today.

Ellis, Joseph J.
▶ *First Family: Abigail and John Adams.* 2010. Knopf. 978-0307269621. 320pp.

Scholar, Pulitzer Prize winner, and best-selling author of books about the characters and events of the American Revolution, Joseph Ellis turns his attention to John and Abigail Adams and their enduring relationship. His goal is to discover how they were able to "sustain their love over a lifetime filled with daunting challenges." War, separations, financial concerns, the births and deaths of children, and the founding of a new country were just some of the events that John and Abigail faced together. Using their letters as the basis of his exploration, Ellis narrates the lives of these two great Americans, their tumultuous times, and the enduring love, respect, and friendship they shared.

Gill, Gillian.
We Two: Victoria and Albert, Rulers, Partners, Rivals. 2009. Ballantine. 978-0345484055. 480pp.

It is one of history's ironies that the parents in the Victorian family that set the standard for propriety were each raised in very dysfunctional families—Queen Victoria in England and her husband Prince Albert in Germany. Each survived a childhood where extreme pressures were placed upon them, where marriage was a dynastic strategy, and tiny children had the weight of kingdoms on their heads. Gill details the family milieu and the evolving relationship of Victoria and Albert in this engrossing story of their lives growing up separately in their odd families and then coming together to negotiate a lasting and loving relationship as an exemplary married couple and the parents of children who would populate the royal houses of Europe. *Victoria's Daughters* (1999) by Jerrold M. Packard looks at the lives of Victoria and Albert's five daughters. *Born to Rule: Five Reigning Consorts, Granddaughters of Queen Victoria* (2005) by Julia P. Gelardi looks at five of their granddaughters.

Kashner Sam and Nancy Schoenberger.
Furious Love: Elizabeth Taylor, Richard Burton, and the Marriage of the Century. 2010. Harper. 006156284X. 512pp.

The tempestuous on and off love story of two larger-than-life personalities, each a star—she on film, he on the stage. When they met, it was instant combustion and their lives became a round of love, lust, booze, obsession, possession, money earned, money spent, children, siblings, marriage, divorce, and marriage and divorce again. Compulsively readable, full of gossipy tidbits about the people who orbited the Burtons, surprisingly gentle about their families, and filled with enough insight to make it feel like more than a guilty-pleasure. This is A-List Hollywood history.

Rowley, Hazel.
Tête-à-Tête: Simone de Beauvoir and Jean Paul Sartre. 2005. Harper. 978-0060520595. 432pp.

From the time they were university students together in the 1920s, until the death of first Sartre, then Beauvoir in the 1980s, these two blazing personalities were locked in a relationship. As lovers, friends, and intellectual soul mates, they stormed through their own lives and the lives of multiple lovers and friends. This is the story of all the relationships. Their milieu and times—the occupation of Paris, the expansion of existentialism, and the rise of feminism—remain secondary to the intense connection of these two 20th-century philosophers.

Frenemies—Thrown Together by History

History is replete with unlikely alliances—figures that because of chance, geography, timing, or circumstances are thrown into company but who under other circumstances would not seek each other out—in other words, frenemies.

Alther, Lisa.
Blood Feud: The Hatfields and McCoys: The Epic Story of Murder and Vengeance. 2012. Lyons Press. 978-0762779185. 304pp.

Neighbors became bitter enemies in the mountains of Kentucky and West Virginia in the epic feud that lasted for generations. Hating each other, killing each other, and sometimes falling in love with each other became a way of life for these large, cantankerous clans in 19th-century Appalachia. Alther writes a rapid-paced story about the people whose names became a cliché for long standing, and to outsiders, almost unfathomable family animosity.

Dobbs, Michael.
One Minute to Midnight: Kennedy, Khrushchev and Castro on the Brink of Nuclear War. 2008. Knopf. 978-1400043583. 426pp.

Over 13 days in October 1962, the Cuban Missile Crisis unfolded and humanity held its breath as the world came closer to fully involved nuclear destruction than ever before or since. Soviet nuclear missile silos being built in Cuba brought the Cold War within striking distance of the United States, and America needed to act. Though they began as belligerents, Kennedy in the White House and Khrushchev in the Kremlin soon realized the madness needed to end, but events seemed to be spiraling away from them. Could they regain control, contain Castro, and step back from the brink? Using new research, conducting more than 100 interviews, and scouring newly declassified film and photographs, Dobbs turns history into a thriller as he narrates the hour-by-hour unfolding of events during this tense moment of Cold War brinkmanship.

Fleischner, Jennifer.
Mrs. Lincoln and Mrs. Keckly: The Remarkable Story of the Friendship between a First Lady and a Former Slave. 2003. Broadway Books. 978-0767902588. 372pp.

Childish, self-absorbed, perhaps mentally ill, Mary Lincoln was a woman who needed help. Strong, practical, and schooled by the hardships of slavery and poverty, Elizabeth Keckly was a woman who could take command. Lizzy Keckly met Mary Lincoln in 1861 when Mrs. Lincoln needed a skilled dressmaker. Their connection (could a relationship between a white woman and a black woman in 1860s America be a friendship?) endured until Keckly wrote a book about her life in slavery and her work with the Lincolns—a book for which she was vilified. Fleischner tells the intriguing story of the unlikely alliance of these two women of very different experience noting that "history has not been kind to Mary Lincoln, but it has neglected Elizabeth Keckly altogether."

Herman, Arthur.
Gandhi and Churchill: The Epic Rivalry that Destroyed an Empire and Forged Our Age. 2008. Bantam. 978-0553804638. 736pp.

The struggle of India to break free from British rule is shown as a battle between two of the 20th century's most colossal personalities: Winston Churchill, the warrior representing the English establishment and imperial continuity, and Mohandas Gandhi, the London-trained, Hindu lawyer steadfast in his philosophy of peaceful resistance. In this panoramic dual biography, Herman tells the story of these two giants, each decidedly sure of his position, each a sincere if flawed man, and both courageous and earnest in their efforts to pursue what they thought was the right path—Gandhi working to free India and achieve total independence for its people, and Churchill fighting to retain valuable India as part of the soon-to-unravel British Empire. An ambitious depiction of two fascinating characters tied together by history.

Jordan, Jonathan W.
Brothers, Rivals, Victors: Eisenhower, Patton, Bradley, and the Partnership that Drove the Allied Conquest in Europe. 2011. NAL. 978-0451232120. 654pp.

"A rich man from southern California, a poor man from the Missouri backwoods, and a middle-class man from middle-class Kansas" become three of the generals responsible for victory in Europe during World War II. Jordan draws heavily on diaries, letters, personal papers, and reminiscences of people who knew these men to tell this fast-paced story about three great Americans who despite their various quirks and issues pulled together to win the war.

Morgan, Robert.
Lions of the West: Heroes and Villains of the Westward Expansion. 2011. Chapel Hill. 978-1565126268. 496pp.

Easy to read, interesting, and informative, Morgan tells the stories of 10 men who moved America west in the years after the revolution and before the Civil War. Morgan shows how the lives of Thomas Jefferson, Andrew Jackson, John Chapman (Johnny Appleseed), Davy Crockett, Sam Houston, James K. Polk, Winfield Scott, Kit Carson, Nicholas Trist, and John Quincy Adams intersected at different moments and how their ideas, hopes, and personalities meshed and clashed. In this book, Morgan acknowledges an historical truth: "Historians may concentrate on the famous, but most of what happens is the composite deeds of common folk. . . . We must consider the 'lions' of the West, but it was the unnoticed thousands on foot and on horseback, in wagons and ox carts, who made the story a fact." A great one-volume compendium of many lives and a large piece of the American story.

Strathern, Paul.
▶ *The Artist, the Philosopher, and the Warrior: The Intersecting Lives of Da Vinci, Machiavelli, and Borgia and the World They Shaped.* 2009. Bantam 978-0553807523. 480pp.

These men comprise "a unique constellation, each in his own way emblematic of a distinct aspect of humanity"—Borgia, intuitive and cunning, but brutal and savage; Leonardo, accomplished and humane, yet enigmatic; and Machiavelli, "by comparison . . . a normal man," but a student of human behavior, power, and political thinking. Strathern argues that the intersection of these three robust and disparate personalities in the Italian Renaissance world of 1502 affected the entire world. Strathern has also written about the Medici, Napoleon, the history of medicine, and multiple philosophers.

A Picture instead of a Thousand Words— Picture Book Biographies

Picture books can distill biography to its essence. Each book in this list is simply written and uniquely illustrated, and offers an author's note providing more information about the subject. Each book is a wonderful read for an adult and even more fun when shared with a child.

Gerstein, Mordicai. ♛
The Man Who Walked between the Towers. 2003. Roaring Brook Press 978-0761317913. 36pp.

On August 7, 1974, as construction on the Twin Towers of the World Trade Center neared completion, a young Frenchman named Philippe Petit walked a tightrope between them in a daring act of artistry. He and a small group of friends secretly strung a wire between the towers in the night. At dawn, Petit stepped out and for almost an hour walked and danced a half mile above the ground. This is a graceful look at an audacious perhaps foolish act of performance art and a gentle reminder of the magnificence of the Towers.

Krull, Kathleen and Paul Brewer. Illustrated by Boris Kulikov.
Fartiste. 2008. Simon and Schuster. 978-1416928287. 40pp.

Joseph Pujol, a music-hall performer in turn-of-the-century France, was a comedian extraordinaire with a singular talent—he farted onstage. Pujol could produce all manner of sounds, from sneezes to themes by Mozart, expelling odorless air from his derriere. He was a sensation. Krull and illustrator Boris Kulikov present a joyful look at this unique artist (whose actual talent was total control of his abdominal muscles) from the past.

Martin, Jacqueline Briggs. Illustrated by Mary Azarian. ♛
Snowflake Bentley. 1998. Houghton Mifflin Books for Children. 978-0395861622. 32pp.

Wilson Bentley, who grew up in Vermont, loved snow. He loved it so much that he spent his life photographing individual snowflakes. Part scientist and part artist, Bentley's work has come down to us as a record of the genuine uniqueness of every snowflake. This lovely book illustrated with colorful woodcuts tells the story of Bentley's passion for snowflakes with quiet, snow-hushed dignity.

McDonnell, Patrick. ♛
▶ *Me . . . Jane.* 2011. Little Brown Books for Young Readers. 978-0316045469. 40pp.

The prim little girl who loves to play outdoors and cherishes her toy monkey, Jubilee, grows up to be Jane Goodall and teaches humanity about our kinship with chimpanzees and nature. This small story shows how a girl's childhood dream became her life's work. This is an exemplary picture book with spare text and whimsical illustrations about a woman who chose an unusual path.

Sis, Peter. ♛
The Wall: Growing up Behind the Iron Curtain. 2007. Farrar, Straus and Giroux. 978-0374347017. 56pp.

This memoir of growing up in Prague in the 1960s is an unusual topic for a picture book. Sis was an artist from birth and he always had a pencil or paintbrush in his hand. But the harsh reality of political oppression and control brought him into conflict with his society, and eventually led him to escape. Using drawings, photos, and excerpts from his diaries, Sis tells what it was like to grow up subjugated to a political system that had no regard for the creativity or intellectual freedom of its citizens.

Sweet, Melissa. ♛
Balloons over Broadway: The True Story of the Puppeteer of Macy's Parade. 2011. Houghton Mifflin Books for Children. 978-0547199450. 40pp.

Tony Sarg was a man who loved to tinker. He drew, he built toys, and he made puppets. Already a well-known illustrator, marionette maker, and performer when he went to work for Macy's in New York City, Sarg used all his talent, experience, and ingenuity to create the monumental floating puppets for the famous Macy's Thanksgiving Day parade. Sweet uses colorful and lively collages to tell the story of Sarg and the origins of the puppets America regards as a holiday tradition.

Watson, Renee. Illustrated by Christian Robinson.
Harlem's Little Blackbird. 2012. Random House Books for Young Readers. 978-0375869730. 40pp.

Florence Mills was the most extraordinary performing artist you never heard of. A figure of the Harlem Renaissance, she was acclaimed in New York and London as a star of great talent and immense kindness. Sadly, no recordings of her singing and no films of her dancing exist. But she is not forgotten, and Watson and Robinson have offered her to a new generation in this sincere depiction of a beloved performer.

The Moneymakers—Famous Capitalists

The application of creativity to commerce is a story that we never tire of hearing and the lives of people with a talent for making and spending money are endlessly intriguing. These are the stories of famous international moneymakers and money spenders.

Bown, Stephen R.
Merchant Kings: When Companies Ruled the World, 1600–1900. 2010. St. Martin's. 978-0312616113. 314pp.

Ambitious, competitive, arrogant, ruthless—all traits that could be applied to the six men whose stories make up this book. Each founded or worked in the service of an early corporation that acted more like a political empire than a business concern. Brown argues that these men were not capitalists as much as monopolists, and each wielded great political and economic power over millions of people. Though ostensibly just merchants trading and selling such commodities as spices, otter pelts, beaver fur, and diamonds, these men and the companies they ruled greatly affected the futures of the countries they plundered and laid much of the groundwork for today's global business world.

Bundles, A'Lelia.
On Her Own Ground: The Life and Times of Madam C.J. Walker. 2001. Scribner. 0684825821. 415pp.

Before Mary Kay, Avon, and Arbonne, Madame C.J. Walker lived a very American rags-to-riches story. Born Sarah Breedlove in 1867 Louisiana, she made herself into an entrepreneur, educator, and social force through the mail order and direct market sales of her hair care and beauty products. Walker left little personal information behind, but Bundles, a descendant of Walker, fills the gaps in Madam Walker's personal story with fascinating social history of African Americans after the Civil War, turn-of-the-century St. Louis, the power of black churches and social groups, the early Harlem Renaissance, and American business history.

D'Antonio, Michael.
A Full Cup: Sir Thomas Lipton's Extraordinary Life and His Quest for the America's Cup. 2010. Riverhead. 159448760X. 368pp.

Relentlessly optimistic and charming, Tommy Lipton rose from poverty to invent the first chain of grocery stores and sail yachts with kings. Growing up in Glasgow, he helped in his parent's small egg and butter shop, but driving ambition and a vision of how to do it better led him to develop stores with great customer service and cheaper goods. Eventually, he became a tea baron (yes, that Lipton) and a competitive sailor. A fun read about an interesting, enigmatic man. D'Antonio is also the author of an intriguing book about America's chocolate king, *Hershey: Milton S. Hershey's Extraordinary Life of Wealth, Empire, and Utopian Dreams* (2007).

Himelstein, Linda.
King of Vodka: The Story of Pyotr Smirnov and the Upheaval of an Empire. 2009. HarperBusiness. 0060855894. 416pp.

When Pyotr Smirnov died in 1898, Russian newspapers called him a "giant of Russian industry"—a remarkable achievement for a man who had been born the son of serfs. His rise to wealth through the successful manufacturing and marketing of one of Russia's most popular vices—vodka—is told with verve by business journalist Himelstein. She follows the family fortunes through his sons with the dramatic history of Imperial Russian's destruction by revolution as the backdrop. For another business success based on imbibing, read *The Widow Clicquot: The Story of a Champagne Empire and the Woman Who Ruled It* (2008) by Tilar J. Mazzeo.

King, Greg.
A Season of Splendor: The Court of Mrs. Astor in Gilded Age New York. 2008. Wiley. 978-0470185698. 528pp.

The real-life characters of the Gilded Age come to life in this book with all their opulence and arrogance on display. King tells all about the Astors and the Vanderbilts, the famous Fifth Avenue mansions, the Newport "cottages," the clothes and jewels, the over-the-top dinner parties and balls, private railway carriages and yachts, the business deals, the marriages, and the society rules they made up and then pressured each other to live by. A comprehensive and absorbing look at the lives of some very wealthy Americans who held sway from 1870 to 1914.

Landes, David S.
Dynasties: Fortunes and Misfortunes of the World's Great Family Businesses. 2006. Viking. 978-0670033386. 384pp.

Defining a dynasty as a family-owned business with three generations of family control, Landes, emeritus Harvard professor of economics, looks at the business lives of famous families in differing realms—banking, Rothschilds and Barings; automobiles, Toyodas, Fords and Agnellis; and wealth from natural resources, Rockefellers and Guggenheims. Landes offers quick sketches in this entertaining and fast-paced book about legendary lineages and their good fortune in business. Landes is best known for his 1999 best seller, *The Wealth and Poverty of Nations: Why Some Are So Rich and Some So Poor.*

Millhauser, Steven. 🏆
Martin Dressler: The Tale of an American Dreamer. 1996. Vintage (paperback). 978-0679781271. 293pp. FICTION

Awarded the Pulitzer Prize for fiction in 1997, this novel disappoints as many readers as it enthralls with its thought-provoking depiction of the pursuit of the American Dream. Martin Dressler is a born merchant and a confident man with a big dream—to build the world's most amazing hotel. Martin has the prerequisites to achieve the American Dream—creative drive, an unstoppable personality, and belief in his own success. But as the dreamer overtakes the practical man of business, the American Dream starts to fail. Is the dream always just out of grasp? Is the dream worth the struggle to achieve it? Millhauser's story is provocative and his evocation of turn-of-the-century New York is satisfying.

Slack, Charles.
Hetty: The Genius and Madness of America's First Female Tycoon. 2004. HarperCollins. 006054256X. 258pp.

In books about the Gilded Age era of Robber Barons, conspicuous consumption and fantastic personal wealth, and the era of Rockefeller, Fisk, Gould, and Carnegie, one name seldom comes up: Hetty Green. Born in 1834 and died in 1916, Hetty Green lived a strange, lonely life. She inherited a family fortune made from whaling and increased her wealth through shrewd, fearless investing that she, unusual at the time, controlled. But while her wealthy compatriots were enjoying their money and eventually refashioning themselves as philanthropists, she remained famous as a miser and a miserable, litigious woman too tightfisted to spend any of her vast wealth. A fascinating character and a book that gives insight into the history of American business from whaling to Wall Street.

Weightman, Gavin.
▶ *The Industrial Revolutionaries: The Making of the Modern World, 1776–1914.* 2007. Grove Press. 978-0802118998. 422pp.

The men who brought us the Industrial Revolution—Marc Isambard Brunel, Sir Henry Bessemer, James Watt, Eli Whitney, and many others—were motivated by a desire to help mankind and make a little money for themselves. Weightman offers multiple portraits of the practical men who earned fame and fortune by making the world modern in this lively social history of the Industrial Revolution.

Gossip or History? You Decide

Fabulous wealth, love and sex, betrayal—constant themes throughout history—and stories that make lively reading. Definitely part of the human story, but where is the line between gossip and history? You decide.

Brown, Tina.
The Diana Chronicles. 2007. Doubleday. 978-0385517089. 542pp.

Young, romantic, beautiful, and fantastically photogenic, Diana Spencer captivated the world when she married Charles, Prince of Wales, in 1981. But the fairy tale was unreal and life became hell for Diana trapped in a loveless marriage, under the thumb of a controlling family. She turned the tables on them however becoming a media superstar and eventually a sacrificial victim. Brown is a smooth stylist and great writer of dishy, tabloidy prose, but she offers some genuine insights into one of the most interesting women of the 20th century. Diana is a character of seemingly endless appeal. *Diana: Her True Story in Her Own Words* (1992) by Andrew Morton and *Diana in Search of Herself: Portrait of a Troubled Princess* (1999) by Sally Bedell Smith also offer interesting perspectives.

Farquhar, Michael.
▶ *A Treasury of Royal Scandals: The Shocking True Stories History's Wickedest, Weirdest, Most Wanton Kings, Queens, Tsars, Popes, and Emperors.* 2001. Penguin. 978-0739420256. 323pp.

These stories of international royals and popes with some ancient Greeks and Romans thrown in—some just naughty, others truly evil, and a few undoubtedly insane—are told with energy and wit in this breezy read that will delight those who like history with a lighter touch. Once you start down this genre road of royal gossip, you may want to keep traveling. For more saucy stories of naughty nobles, see *Royal Babylon: The Alarming History of European Royalty* (2001) by Karl Shaw, and *Sex with Kings: 500 Years of Adultery, Power, Rivalry, and Revenge* (2005) and *Sex with the Queen: 900 Years of Vile Kings, Virile Lovers, and Passionate Politics* (2007) both by Eleanor Herman.

Fraser, Antonia.
Love and Louis XIV: The Women in the Life of the Sun King. 2006. Nan Talese. 978-0385509848. 416pp.

Shed no tears for the Sun King—his life was full of love. From his mother through his wives, mistresses, wards, and daughters-in-law, Louis was surrounded by women who cherished him and did all they could to please him, to fill his days with comfort and ease, and to entertain and amuse him for his entire long life. The French royal court is on full display in this book. Fraser is a master at historical narrative and the personal lives of the rich and royal are her realm. Her breakthrough book *Mary, Queen of Scots* (1969) is still an excellent read.

Gordon, Meryl.
Mrs. Astor Regrets: The Hidden Betrayals of a Family beyond Reproach. 2008.
Houghton Mifflin. 978-0618893737. 336pp.

In 2006, Brooke Astor's grandson sued his father, Astor's only child, al-
leging mistreatment of his then 103-year-old grandmother, the famous philanthropist and social charmer. This is the story of Mrs. Astor's fabulous life, her
final days and the family, and ultimately legal battle over her estate. Follow
up with Astor's charming memoir of her unusual childhood, *Patchwork Child*
(originally published in 1961 and reissued in 1993) and Frances Kiernan's *The
Last Mrs. Astor: A New York Story* (2007).

Graham, Laurie.
Gone with the Windsors. 2006. HarperCollins. 978-0060872717. 403 pp.
FICTION

In the 1930s, American widow Maybell Brumby—a fun-loving, curvy
blonde, wealthy, good-hearted, and somewhat dim—takes up residence in
London and renews her schoolgirl friendship with Wallis Simpson. Maybell
shines in the world of cocktail trolleys, weekend house parties, Ascot, sum-
mers at Biarritz, and orbit around the minor royals just as Wallis is laying siege
to HRH, the Duke of Windsor. It's frothy fun and a fast-paced mix of fact and
fiction as Maybell recounts all in her diary.

MacColl, Gail and Carol McD. Wallace.
To Marry an English Lord. 2012 (originally published in 1989). Workman Publishing Company (paperback). 978-0761171959. 416pp. ⓎⒶ

A colorful and comprehensive look at the 19th-century phenomenon of
wealthy Gilded Age American heiresses marrying broke English aristocrats.
Rich Americans wanted titles and class, while bankrupt English lords needed
money and new bloodlines: Vanderbilts, Astors, and Jeromes, all sent daughters; in fact, more than 100 young American women entered into this matrimo-
nial fray. This book originally published in 1989 and reissued to take advantage
of the *Downton Abbey* phenomenon is a delightful light read with great illustrations and lots of sidebars.

McLain, Paula.
The Paris Wife: A Novel. 2011. Ballantine. 978-0345521309. 336pp. FICTION

Two passionate people fall in love, marry, and move to Paris to live a life
of freedom and creativity. Hadley Richardson—an intelligent, uncomplicated
woman—wants to love well, be comfortable and happy, support her husband's
dream, and raise a family. But the man she shares this journey with is Ernest
Hemingway. He is young, ambitious, vibrant, and struggling to make his mark.
The relationship of these two people is on a crash course to failure. McLain
dramatizes the interpersonal world of Hadley, Ernest, and their talented set of
friends in this recent best seller about love and the "Lost Generation."

Chapter Three

Setting

When you read, do you seek a rich sense of geography or an understanding of the details of daily life from a specific era of the past? Readers who like a strong sense of setting will find books in these lists that satisfy their cravings for a strong evocation of a place or a time period.

History readers have already stated their first setting preference—the past. But the past is a monumental landscape of land and water, home and abroad, and public and private spheres. The books in these lists offer immersion into the classical world of ancient Greece and Rome, the darkness of a prehistoric cave, the Mississippi River, the Old West, the chaos of declining empires, and the rush and excitement of New York's Times Square and Metropolitan Museum of Art.

Pilgrims on a Journey

Throughout history, many have sought spiritual places for solace, for penance, or for a deeper knowledge of the world or of one's self. These books offer an exploration of some of the world's spiritual settings and famous pilgrimage sites.

Eck, Diana.
India: A Sacred Geography. 2012. Harmony Books. 978-0385531900. 559pp.
>   The vast space on the map that we call a unified country of India is really a territory where every forest, river, and mountain is linked to a myth, where every religious site is the center of someone's spiritual universe, and where the entire landscape is crisscrossed with "tracks of pilgrimage." Eck, a renowned scholar of comparative religion and Indian studies, takes us on a

journey through the vibrant complexity of past and present India to show how the sacred abides there.

Feiler, Bruce.
▶ *Where God Was Born: A Journey by Land to the Roots of Religion.* 2005. William Morrow. 0060574879. 416pp.

"The collision of politics, geography, and faith has dominated nearly every story in the Middle East since the birth of writing." Feiler, a Jew from the American South, answers an internal call to visit the locales of the Old Testament and experience the reality of the stories passed down to us in the Bible. "The calling wasn't religious exactly; it was historical, archaeological, cultural." Feiler reprises the formula that made his 2001 book *Walking the Bible* a best seller with his exploration of contemporary politics, ancient history, religious questioning, arduous travel, and a sincere and humble search for understanding.

Harris, Ruth.
Lourdes: Body and Spirit in the Secular Age. 1999. Viking. 0670879053. 474pp.

The French Pyrenean town of Lourdes became a world pilgrimage site after 1858 when a poor 14-year-old shepherdess named Bernadette had several sightings of the Virgin Mary at a rugged, hard-to-access mountain grotto previously used by locals as an illicit pasturing place for cows and pigs. Since the sighting, the sick and infirm have traveled to Lourdes hoping for the Virgin's intersession on their behalf. In this beautifully written and rigorously documented book, Harris approaches an intensely religious subject as an objective and unbiased historian hoping to "create a bridge between scholarship and the general reader."

Hitt, Jack.
Off the Road: A Modern Day Walk down the Pilgrim's Route into Spain. 2005 (originally published in 1994). Simon and Schuster (paperback). 978-0743261111. 272pp.

Humorous but not irreverent, Hitt walked the Camino de Santiago de Compostela, the 500-mile pilgrims path in northwestern Spain that typically starts in France and ends at the medieval Cathedral to St. John at Compostela. Hitt comments on the history he encounters as well as his copilgrims and the inner experience of the arduous and life-change walk along The Way.

Wolfe, Michael.
One Thousand Roads to Mecca: Ten Centuries of Travelers Writing about the Muslim Pilgrimage. 1997. Grove. 978-0802135995. 656pp.

Islam is a religion that offers a unifying experience to its international adherents, the requirement of a once-in-a-lifetime pilgrimage to Mecca—birthplace of Muhammad, holiest city in Islam, and the site of the revelation of the Koran. This compilation of excerpts from the personal travel accounts of 23 pilgrims over the last 1,000 years offers a glimpse of the religious rituals and the arduous travel undertaken by Muslim faithful and forbidden to those not members of the Islamic religion. Wolfe, a convert to Islam, has also made the journey and written about it in his book *The Hadj: An American's Pilgrimage to Mecca* (1993).

Decline and Fall—The Passage of Empires

All empires fall, even after thousands of years of splendor. If you seek a broad examination of a place and a way of life that is no more, these books are for you.

Brendon, Piers.
The Decline and Fall of the British Empire, 1781–1997. 2008. Knopf 978-0307268297. 786pp.

Brendon, historian and Cambridge Fellow, offers a "momentous saga" in detailing the "decline and fall of (to employ the inescapable cliché) the greatest empire that the world has ever seen." He argues that the vast, paternalistic British Empire was in decline for 200 years, starting with the loss of the America colonies and ending with the peaceful though regretted handover of Hong Kong to China. The British did provide infrastructure, education, security, and organization to its colonies, but was also the force behind the Opium Wars, the Irish Famine, the Indian Mutiny, the Boer War, the "morass" of the Middle East and Palestine, the Mau Mau uprising in Kenya, and the Falkland War. This is a richly written history, detailed but also lush and large, about the inevitable, even if prolonged, end of Empire.

Brownworth, Lars.
▶ *Lost to the West: The Forgotten Byzantine Empire that Rescued Western Civilization.* 2009. Crown. 978-0307407955. 352pp.

The western portion of the Roman Empire may have fallen, but Rome continued in the East—the Byzantine Empire picked up and ruled the Christian world for another 1,000 years until it was the Ottoman Empire's turn. Brownworth presents 1,000 years of military, religious, and social tumult by looking at the Byzantine world through the lives and actions of its rulers. Amiable and conversational Brownworth is a high-school history teacher whose podcast "12 Byzantine Rulers" became a sensation and led to this book. If the Byzantine world captures you, read *Sailing from Byzantium: How a Lost Empire Shaped the World* (2006) by Colin Wells.

Crowley, Roger.
City of Fortune: How Venice Ruled the Seas. 2012. Random House. 978-1400068203. 464pp.

Venice has always been an unusual place, part Europe and part East, part sea part land, part city part nation, a world poised between commerce and art, between Byzantine emperors and Roman popes. But from the 11th to the 17th centuries, Venice was very clearly defined as the wealthiest city in the world. Home to a population of natural merchants and traders who relished the profits to be made at sea, Venice was a launching point for several Crusades and a natural nexus for the spice trade from the East. Crowley shows how Venice once conquered and ruled, but eventually fell. This is the final book in Crowley's loosely structured Mediterranean trilogy that includes *Empires of the Sea* (2008) and *1453* (2005).

Davies, Norman.
Vanished Kingdoms: The Rise and Fall of States and Nations. 2012. Viking 978-0670022731. 803pp.

Burgundia, Aragon, Galicia, Etruria, the USSR—where are they now? The people and the locales still exist, but the states disappeared, why? Calling his book sober but not pessimistic, Davies offers the histories of 15 European states, kingdoms, or dynasties that once were but are no more. This book is brilliant, both traditional and quirky, and Davies, renowned scholar of European history, offers an unusual way to look at both the present and the past. Generously filled with maps, illustrations, and family trees.

Goodwin, Jason.
Lords of the Horizons: A History of the Ottoman Empire. 2003. Picador (paperback). 978-0312420666. 368pp.

From the 1300s to the early years of the 20th century, the vast Ottoman Empire spanned the known world joining East and West and governed by absolute rulers from its magnificent capitol, Constantinople. Successor to the Byzantine Empire, it is said that the Ottoman Empire peaked in 1566 and was in decline for the next 400 years. Goodwin offers a look at this exotic lost world in this somewhat anecdotal, poetic, and enthralling read. Goodwin is also the author of a series of evocative mysteries set in Istanbul that feature Yashim the Eunuch.

MacQuarrie, Kim.
The Last Days of the Incas. 2007. Simon and Schuster. 978-0743260497. 522pp.

The Inca Empire was the largest empire in pre-Columbian South America. It provided a basic standard of living for its people, cities with broad streets and irrigation systems, an economy based upon agriculture, a refined society that created golden tableware and beautifully woven textiles, and a governmental structure based on organization and good management that insured its citizens sufficient food, clothing, and shelter. Of course, there were also taxes, wars, and human sacrifice, but still, the Incans controlled a vast empire that ended in the 1530s when the Conquistadors, led by Pizarro, conquered and destroyed it. MacQuarrie writes a compelling and detailed narrative about the end of the Incan Empire.

Tourist Traps

Packing the family into the station wagon and seeing America this summer? You'll want to do some background reading first. Brush up on the history of some of America's major travel destinations with these books.

Berton, Pierre.
Niagara: A History of the Falls. 1997 (first published in 1992). Kodansha International. 1568361548. 371pp.

A geological marvel formed by glaciers, the Niagara Falls are three distinct waterfalls that lie on the border between Canada and the United States. Not especially high, but very wide, the falls have long enticed tourists and lured adventure seekers—especially tightrope walkers and barrel riders—with their awesome beauty and sheer power. Popular Canadian historian Berton gives a very detailed look at the history and grandeur of the falls.

Gross, Michael.
Rogues' Gallery: The Secret Story of the Lust, Lies, Greed, and Betrayals that Made the Metropolitan Museum of Art. 2009. Broadway Books. 978-0767924887. 545pp.

With a collection of more than 2 million objects that were created over 5,000 years, housed in a complex of buildings that occupy 2 million square feet on 13 acres of land in New York's Central Park, and visited by 4.6 million people a year, the Met, by all measurements, is huge. And it took huge personalities with huge egos and outsized bank accounts to create it. Gross acknowledges that his gossipy book is unauthorized, but that makes this an even more enticing guilty-pleasure read about one of the world's greatest art museums.

Pauketat, Timothy R.
Cahokia: Ancient America's Great City on the Mississippi. 2009. Viking. 978-0670020904. 194pp.

If you travel to St. Louis, Missouri, cross the Mississippi into Illinois and visit the Cahokia Mounds State Park. The mounds are the remnants of a once populous city that housed pyramids, plazas, temples, and astronomical observatories. Modernization, highways, and urban growth razed most of the ancient mounds, but archaeologists still seek to understand the mysteries of this early Mississippian culture that practiced human sacrifice, built an elaborate city, and whose inhabitants had, by about 1400, disappeared. Pauketat lucidly presents the evidence in this brief work about the prehistoric American World Heritage site.

Poole, Robert M.
On Hallowed Ground: The Story of Arlington National Cemetery. 2009. Walker and Company. 978-0802715487. 352pp.

Once the gracious home of Robert E. Lee and his wife, the great grand-daughter of Martha Washington, Arlington became a cemetery during the Civil War when a portion of Lee's property was confiscated as a burial place for the overflow of war dead in Washington D.C. Poole traces the evolution of Arlington from its Civil War beginnings to the present day discussing the people, rituals, and meaning of this special place. This is a somber and beautiful book about where and how we honor those who have served America.

Starr, Kevin.
▶ *Golden Gate: The Life and Times of America's Greatest Bridge.* 2010. Bloomsbury Press. 978-1596915343. 215pp.

Emotion, imagination, and engineering—all were needed to create the Golden Gate Bridge, symbol of San Francisco, California, and the American West. Constructed between 1933 and 1937, it was once the longest suspension bridge in the world (currently, it ranks ninth). Starr lyrically explains the design, engineering, and building of the bridge; the politics of its creation; the appearances of the bridge in popular culture; artistic details like its Art Deco style and unexpected color (International Orange); and its role as the farewell point for suicides. This is an elegant, extended essay of praise to the magnificence of the Golden Gate Bridge.

Traub, James.
The Devil's Playground: A Century of Pleasure and Profit in Times Square. 2004. Random House. 0375507884. 313pp.

Seedy, squalid, and scummy—Times Square has had a reputation. A major intersection in the heart of New York City's theater district, Times Square has been home to shady businesses and sex from the days of the Florodora Girls and Ziegfeld's follies to Runyonesque characters in speakeasies, peep shows, and the 1970s porn super shops. But it has also been a center of creativity: writers, show business, commerce, and communications have all flourished there. Visit Times Square through Traub's vibrant view of a civic space that advertises America to the world and that has rebranded itself from sordid to family-friendly.

The Grand Tour—International Tourist Sites Not to Be Missed

In times past, the capstone of a young gentleman's education was a visit to the world's cultural sites. A trip to historic sites, even as an armchair traveler, can still add a finishing touch offering readers a broader picture of the history of man and the world.

Cornwell, Bernard.
Stonehenge: A Novel of 2000 BC. 2000. Harper. 978-0060197001. 448pp. FICTION
> Alone and almost isolated in the wide open, the megaliths of Stonehenge sit on a flat wide plain 90 miles west of London. The same questions arise for everyone seeing Stonehenge: Who made it? How did they do it? And why? Best-selling author Cornwell offers a version of what could be the truth in this fictional account of the ancient British pagans who built, battled, and sacrificed at Stonehenge. In recent years, Cornwell, better known for his series of novels set during the Napoleonic Wars, has been exploring the foundations of Britain in his <u>Saxon Chronicles</u> series starting with *The Last Kingdom* (2005).

Jones, Nigel.
The Tower: An Epic History of the Tower of London. 2012. St. Martin's Press. 978-0312622961. 456pp.
> First stop on many a London tourist itinerary, the Tower of London is now home to the Royal Jewels, Beefeaters, and tourist kitsch. But for the bulk of its almost 1,000-year history, the tower has been awash in blood. Commissioned by William the Conqueror and designed by a cleric named Gundulf, it was used by British rulers until World War II as a holding pen for prisoners, traitors, spies, wayward royal family members, and—most poignantly—sometimes the innocent. Jones tells the sad and gruesome stories of those who resided, suffered, and died in the tower, and includes an appendix detailing some of the tower's more memorable ghosts.

Man, John.
The Great Wall: The Extraordinary Story of China's Wonder of the World. 2008. Da Capo Press. 978-0306817670. 335pp.
> The Great Wall of China is not really one continuous well-formed wall, but rather sections and pieces that cross the Chinese landscape. Some sections are tourist hot spots, but others sections are impediments to quotidian local undertakings like agriculture and transportation. Author John Man blends personal observations from his own travels, historical research, and a conversational style to debunk the myths (no, you cannot see the Great Wall from space) and offer a current view of the monument. Man is a popularizer of Chinese and Mongolian history and has also written about Genghis Khan, Attila the Hun, and the great Chinese Terra Cotta Army.

Martines, Lauro.
April Blood: Florence and the Plot against the Medici. 2004. Oxford (paperback). 978-0195176094. 320pp.
> A major stop on Grand Tours of previous eras was Florence, Italy, birthplace of the Renaissance. Renowned scholar Martines offers the "bloody tale" of the Pazzi Conspiracy of 1478 when Florence's other prominent families tried to murder the powerful Medici and replace them as rulers. When the

conspiracy failed, the gory reprisals began. In this brilliant look at a brutal time, Martines provides the drama and sensationalism of a 21st-century best seller while using recent scholarship to elucidate the complex politics and the colorful personalities of Renaissance Florence.

Preston, Diana and Michael Preston.
▶ *Taj Mahal: Passion and Genius at the Heart of the Moghul Empire.* 2007. Walker and Company. 978-0802715111. 317pp.

While the Pilgrims struggled to survive in America and the Thirty Years War dragged on in Europe, a ruler in India began to build a tomb for his beloved, recently deceased wife. In 1632, Shah Jahan started the project that took almost 30 years and an unaccounted amount of wealth to complete. In easy-reading prose and well-documented scholarship, the Prestons offer a family drama, a sweeping dynastic story, and the architectural and design history of this famous building considered by many to be the world's most sublime monument to lost love.

The Wild, Wild West

The Old West, the Wild West, or the American Frontier—a setting of vastness, adventure, courage, suffering, and human drama. These are stories set west of the Mississippi, as newcomers were making the final push west battling elements, displacing native peoples, and populating the immense area of America.

Brown, Daniel.
The Indifferent Stars Above: The Harrowing Saga of a Donner Party Bride. 2009. William Morrow. 0061348104. 352pp.

The overwhelming rigors of the Western trail, the unforgiving Sierra Mountains, and the personalities of the hard-pressed pioneers are vividly depicted in this spellbinding version of the famous incident of the Donner Party. You may know how the story ends, but Brown is an enthralling writer and spares no detail in his narrative of the luckless party who reached the mountains too late in the season of 1846–1847. Another great read of the same story is *Desperate Passage: The Donner Party's Perilous Journey West* (2008) by Ethan Rarick.

Dolnick, Edward.
Down the Great Unknown: John Wesley Powell's 1869 Journey of Discovery & Tragedy. 2001. Harper Collins. 978-0965334181. 384pp.

In 1869, John Wesley Powell, explorer, scientist, and veteran who had lost his right arm in the Civil War, took nine men and four wooden boats on an expedition to explore and map the Grand Canyon. The Colorado River could be ferocious, the canyon walls were fearsome, and knowledge about what they would find was nonexistent. Even though Powell and his men were "immeasurably more rugged than modern travelers" and Powell himself was supremely courageous, strong-willed, and confident, success was not guaranteed. Dolnick has written an exciting, you-are-there book about the treacherous three-month journey.

Guinn, Jeff.

The Last Gunfight: The Real Story of the Shootout at the O.K. Corral— And How It Changed the American West. 2011. Simon and Schuster. 978-1439154243. 392pp.

The shoot-out between the Earp brothers, Doc Holliday, and the Clantons became an iconic event that through subsequent retellings and misinterpretations helped contribute to the myth of the West. Guinn sees the gunfight as a moment when social, economic, and political forces were converging to change the West though the participants didn't know it at the time. His story is full of the personalities and frontier dynamics involved, with a strong sense of setting and a broader analysis of the changing idea of the West. For another take on the story, read *Doc: A Novel* (2011) by Maria Doria Russell.

Gwynne, S.C.

Empire of the Summer Moon: Quanah Parker and the Rise and Fall of the Comanches, the Most Powerful Indian Tribe in American History. 2010. Scribner. 978-1416591054. 384pp.

Quanah Parker was the last chief of the Comanche tribe. His mother, a white woman, had been taken captive as a girl by the Comanche. When Quanah was still a boy, she was recaptured and held against her will by her white family until her early death. Quanah Parker went on to be a warrior and then a peaceful leader who straddled the white and native worlds. Gwynne vividly depicts the brutality of the Texas frontier, the history of the Comanche tribe, and the family whose story became history.

Holliday, J.S.

The World Rushed In: The California Gold Rush Experience. 2002 (originally published in 1981). University of Oklahoma Press (paperback). 978-0806134642. 568pp.

After gold was found in California in 1849, more than 30,000 prospectors rushed to the state hoping to get rich quick and then return home. This is the story of all of those men told through the experiences of one of those men. Holliday offers a firsthand account using the letters and diaries of William Swain, from New York State, who rushed in with the crowd and diligently recorded the journey. By supplementing Swain's descriptive writings with diaries and letters written by other prospectors, Holliday creates a complete picture of the years of the gold rush and the experiences of being on the trail, in the camps, and back home where family waited. A unique book and a history classic. H.W. Brands also tells the story of the gold rush in *The Age of Gold: The California Gold Rush and the New American Dream* (2002).

Sides, Hampton.
▶ *Blood and Thunder: The Epic Story of Kit Carson and the Conquest of the American West.* 2001. Doubleday. 978-0385507776. 480pp.

Epic and sweeping are words that could easily be applied to this story of the settling of the American Southwest between about 1840 and 1870. Sides uses Kit Carson to anchor the narrative, but he interweaves the lives and exploits of many prominent Western figures and he doesn't shy away from the brutality of the westward expansion, the destruction of native ways of life, and the hardships endured by mountain men and pioneer women. A big picture view of the move west.

Williams, John.
Butcher's Crossing. 2007 (originally published in 1960). NYRB Classics (paperback). 978-1590171981. 274pp. FICTION

Will Andrews, a soft easterner with three years of Harvard behind him, decides to fund a buffalo hunt that takes four men on a journey from Kansas into the Colorado Rockies in search of one last great herd. This powerful story sparingly told is an engrossing exploration of the changing ecology and economics of the American West and of the psychology of men who would risk everything for the kill. This book is an underappreciated classic.

That Was the Year That Was

History books can cover millennia or just a single event. These books look at the story of just one year.

Bellesiles, Michael A.
1877: America's Year of Living Violently. 2010. The New Press. 978-1595584410. 386pp.

The Library of Congress subject headings assigned to this book give an idea of what to expect—Social Conflict, Violence, Race Relations, Economic Conditions, and Railroad Strike. Bellesiles's book is densely packed with the events and personalities of a tumultuous year when America took another step forward in its evolution. Bellesiles easily makes his argument that 1877 was a violent year and fully documents how glad Americans were when it was over.

Blom, Philipp.
The Vertigo Years: Europe, 1900–1914. 2008. Basic Books. 978-0465011162. 488pp.

Change and anxiety were rampant in Europe in the early years of the 20th century. We know the anxiety was well warranted, but those living in the time had no notion of the social changes, human destruction, and political turmoil on the horizon. Blom examines each year from 1900 to 1914 looking at different trends, themes, and personalities showing a world that was beginning to move more quickly and perhaps less controllably than ever before. A dense social and cultural history beautifully written as are Blom's other works like *To Have and to Hold: An Intimate History of Collectors and Collecting* (2003).

Howarth, David.
1066: The Year of the Conquest. 1981 (originally published in 1977). Penguin (paperback). 978-0140058505. 208pp.
   This classic work of historical writing takes us to England, Normandy, and Norway in the famous year when William conquered, Harold was killed, and the future of England was recast. In fluid prose that will engage the casual reader, Howarth sets the milieu, describes the events and personalities, addresses the facts and the legends, and surmises the contemporary psychology of the year of Stamford Bridge and Hastings. For a look at England before 1066, read *The Year 1000: What Life Was Like at the Turn of the First Millennium, An Englishman's World* (1999) by Robert Lacey.

Kurlansky, Mark.
▶ *1968: The Year that Rocked the World.* 2004. Ballantine Books. 0345455819. 441pp.
   "There has never been a year like 1968, and it is unlikely that there will ever be one again." From Vietnam to Chicago, from Paris to Prague, the world was alive with unscripted and loosely organized rebellions. The rawness of television, still new and somewhat uncontrolled, added to the foment, as did poetry, drugs, rock and roll, the rise of a youth culture, and the universal human will toward greater freedom. Kurlansky, a master of narrative nonfiction (read *Cod* and *Salt*) has crafted a satisfying montage of a year when reality shifted.

Lee, Christopher.
1603: The Death of Queen Elizabeth I, the Return of the Black Plague, the Rise of Shakespeare, Piracy, Witchcraft and the Birth of the Stuart Era. 2003. St. Martin's. 0312321392. 368pp.
   A list of momentous years might not include 1603, more is the pity argues author Christopher Lee. Focusing on England, Lee shows how 1603 was a major year of transition that saw the death of Elizabeth I ending 117 years of Tudor reign and the start of the Stuart line. 1603 also saw the death of 40,000 British citizens from plague, the continued creative productions of Ben Jonson, William Shakespeare and other poets, as well as a major witch hunt propagated by the king himself. Lee offers an intriguing look at Britain in a year usually given little attention.

Phillips, Kevin.
1775: A Good Year for Revolution. 2012. Penguin. 978-0670025121. 628pp.
   The 20th century had an excessive attraction to 1776 as the "moral and ideological starting point" of the United States. Phillips intended this volume to argue that 1775 was equally as important as 1776, but concluded by

convincing himself that 1775 was an even more important year! The entire English-speaking world was being realigned and the disturbance in the American Colonies was just one of many revolutionary changes.

On the Briny—Stories Set at Sea

What is it about the sea that draws readers again and again? Is it men against the elements? Adventure into the unknown? The complex but beautiful ships? Read these diverse books set on the briny to learn for yourself why stories set at sea have such appeal.

Bown, Stephen R.
Scurvy: How a Surgeon, a Mariner and a Gentleman Solved the Greatest Mystery of the Age of Sail. 2004. Thomas Dunne Books. 978-0312313913. 256pp.

The 18th-century British navy was a dangerous place full of battles, shipwrecks, and drowning, but the greatest danger was scurvy. Vitamin C deficiency caused by the sailors' monotonous diet of salt meat, weevil-ridden biscuit, and an absence of fruits and vegetables led to more naval deaths than warfare. Scurvy had long haunted the world's sailors and the solution baffled great minds for years. In this satisfying chronicle about the dangers of life at sea in the great age of sail, Bown tells how scurvy was conquered and argues convincingly that the disease and its eventual eradication affected history.

Cordingly, David.
▶ *Under the Black Flag: The Romance and the Reality of Life among the Pirates.* 1995. Random House. 0679425608. 296pp.

Popularly depicted as romantic outlaws, often wronged aristocrats, educated, and urbane, the historical truth about pirates is less noble—violent, treacherous young men, driven by the lure of plunder, and abetted by drink. A pirate's career was brutishly short and typically ended in a fight, a drowning, or a hanging. Cordingly takes a thematic approach and looks at the real life of pirates around the world from about the 1500s to modern day. Vibrantly written, includes a helpful glossary of sea terms.

Jensen, Carsten.
We, the Drowned. 2011. Houghton Mifflin Harcourt. 978-0151013777. 688pp.
FICTION

Since the days of the Vikings, the Danes have been masters of the sea. Jensen tells the story of a small town on an island off the coast of Denmark where the men are eternally lured to the water and the women stay on land and endure. Following the islanders from 1848 through World War II is epic and thrilling. This international best seller can easily stand alongside other great seafaring novels like *Moby Dick*, the <u>Horatio Hornblower</u> series, and the *Master and Commander* books.

Nichols, Peter.

Oil and Ice: A Story of Arctic Disaster and the Rise and Fall of America's Last Waling Dynasty. 2010 (originally published in hardback under the title *Final Voyage*). Penguin (paperback). 0143118366. 304pp.

New Bedford Massachusetts was a town devoted to one industry—whaling. Nichols tells of the end of this industry and the final voyage of 32 ships that were trapped in the Arctic in 1872—miraculously all on board, 1,218 men, women, and children, survived. The realities of shipboard life, the business of whaling, and the pain and anxiety of leaving family to make a dangerous living are all narrated with great compassion. For more adventures of life aboard a whaler, read Eric Dolin's *Leviathan: The History of Whaling in America* (2008) and Nathaniel Philbrick's *In the Heart of the Sea: The Tragedy of the Whaleship Essex* (2000).

Toll, Ian W.

Six Frigates: The Epic History of the Founding of the U.S. Navy. 2006. Norton. 978-0393058475. 560pp.

The politics and practicalities of building America's first naval ships are explored in this scholarly but adventure-filled book. Jefferson, Adams, and Madison debated for years about the need for an American navy. But, how could the U.S. government protect merchants and citizens without it? Toll details the treachery of the Barbary pirates, the battle of Tripoli, and the War of 1812 when America's nascent navy "shocked and humbled" Britain's far superior fleet. Toll is a vibrant writer and this book is a great example of academic thought and resources shared in a popular and exciting style.

Wolff, Geoffrey.

The Hard Way Around: The Passages of Joshua Slocum. 2010. Knopf. 978-1400043422. 240pp.

Joshua Slocum lived more at sea than on land in his 65 years. Slocum was a confident man, a father and husband, a natural trader and merchant, a sailor, an adventurer and ultimately a loner, and a figure of romance and questionable judgment. Wolff details the end of the great age of sail and the life and adventures of one of its last large personalities. He gives equal attention to Slocum's stalwart and spirited wife Virginia, who, until her early death, accompanied him and raised their four children onboard their ships. Wolff quotes often from Slocum's own classic *Sailing Alone around the World* (1899) and other contemporary sources like Joseph Conrad and the biography of Slocum written by his eldest son Victor.

Pre, Proto, and Paleo—The World Before History

Our understanding of the world of cavemen and mammoths is pieced together by scientists, historians, and authors using stones and bones, pieces of pots, conjecture, and best guesses. Here are some titles that explore the world when humankind was young and History had yet to be invented.

Auel, Jean.
Clan of the Cave Bear. 2001 (originally published in 1980). Crown. 978-0609610978. 468pp. FICTION

After losing her parents in an earthquake, Ayla is taken in by the medicine woman of another band of people. But Ayla, smaller and a more creative thinker, is always different from her adopted tribe. First-rate storyteller Auel serves up a research supported vision of the time when Cro-Magnons and Neanderthals coexisted in this best-selling blockbuster that continues to capture readers. First in the Earth's Children series that includes *The Valley of the Horses* (1982), *The Mammoth Hunters* (1985), *The Plains of Passage* (1990), *The Shelters of Stone* (2002), and *The Land of the Painted Caves* (2011).

Curtis, Gregory.
The Cave Painters: Probing the Mysteries of the World's First Artists. 2006. Knopf. 978-1400043484. 288pp.

Who struggled into dark, recessed corners of caves in France and Spain 30,000–40,000 years ago to create paintings of large animals running? How did they create the work? What did the paintings mean to them—hunting magic, fertility enhancer, religious icons, or aesthetic decoration? Curtis writes an enthralling story about the cave paintings and the modern scholars, artists, bored kids, and professional adventurers who uncovered them and have tried to understand the meaning of the pictures and the thinking of the prehistoric artists.

Fagan, Brian.
Cro-Magnon: How the Ice Age Gave Birth to the First Modern Humans. 2010. Bloomsbury. 978-1596915824. 320pp.

This narrative account of Cro-Magnons, the first modern humans, includes sidebars containing the more technical information like radiocarbon dating, mitochondrial DNA, and blade technology ("or the Cro-Magnon Swiss Army Knife"). Fagan often uses the phrase "what we now know" indicating that prehistory is a continually evolving field of study as new technologies offer expanding ways to look at the past and more artifacts continue to be found. Fascinating and friendly, Fagan is a master at taking complex data and making a story.

Gibbons, Ann.
The First Human: The Race to Discover Our Earliest Ancestors. 2006. Double-day. 0385512260. 306pp.

Paleoanthropology, the search for and study of human fossils, is a "contentious" field full of strong personalities and political maneuvering. Gibbons, a science writer, has followed the story for decades and tells a good tale of the dust, digging, in-fighting, triumphs, and personal and national politics involved in uncovering the evidence of our earliest African ancestors. As she says, "science lurches forward despite the foibles of the individual scientists." Includes helpful supplemental information like a glossary, bibliography, map, and timeline.

Wade, Nicholas.
Before the Dawn: Recovering the Lost History of Our Ancestors. 2006. Penguin. 978-1594200793. 320pp.

The human species has walked the earth for 2.5 million years, but recorded history only goes back to about 5,000 BC. What was going on before man learned to self-reflect and write everything down? If you go back far enough, history becomes biology and the study of the human genome, only possible since about 2003, can now offer insights into man's deep past. This complex biological material becomes intelligible and intriguing through Wade's clear thinking and lucid prose. An excellent companion piece to Wade's book is Richard Dawkin's *The Ancestor's Tale: A Pilgrimage to the Dawn of Evolution* (2004) that traces humanity back to bacterial ancestors.

Wrangham, Richard.
Catching Fire: How Cooking Made Us Human. 2009. Basic Books. 978-0465013623. 320pp.

Cooking makes food safer and tastier, reduces spoilage, and affects its nutritional makeup allowing human bodies to extract more usable energy. Wrangham argues that harnessing fire and learning to cook gave early humans the needed nutritional boost to become what we are today—upright, large brained, tool making, and language using. Wrangham is a biological anthropologist, and this book tends toward the scientific and anthropological, but his examination of the relationships between fire, cooking, and the evolution of our species is a stimulating work.

Wynn, Thomas and Frederick L. Coolidge.
▶ *How to Think Like a Neandertal.* 2011. Oxford. 978-0199742820. 210pp.

Did Neandertals tell jokes? Did they dream? Were they better adapted to cold and injury than *Homo sapiens*? What did they eat? Why did they disappear? Wynn and Coolidge take the sparse material left over from Neandertal lives and analyze it to present their understanding of the Neandertal mind. Part science and part educated speculation, this is an utterly fascinating examination of our prehistoric cousins and the world they could not master.

Be It Ever So Humble—The History of House and Home

So much of the story of human history takes place on public stages—the battlefield or palace, the town square, cathedral, and halls of government, but these books tell about the other place where history happens—in the privacy of home.

Bryson, Bill.
▶ *At Home: A Short History of Private Life.* 2010. Doubleday. 978-0767919388. 512pp.

> With his trademark wit and gentle spirit, Bryson takes a tour of his home, an aging parsonage in England, and uses his wandering as a way to look at the history of all things domestic—the attic, the cellar, the fuse box, and the staircases, all surprisingly lead to explorations of the history of cemeteries, the historic dangers of childbirth, the prevalence of linen and hemp as fabric throughout history, the Great Exhibition of 1851, and more. You cannot predict what paths Bryson will follow as he rambles through the house and 10,000 years of human domesticity. Lucy Worsley's *If Walls Could Talk: An Intimate History of the Home* (2012) continues along the same lines.

Carter, W. Hodding.
Flushed: How the Plumber Saved Civilization. Atria Books. 2007. 978-0743474092. 256pp. ⓎⒶ

> An offbeat look at an event we all participate in—going potty. Carter's own slight obsession with plumbing leads him on a light-hearted tour of the evolution of the toilet and the history of plumbing and sewage from ancient aqueducts to London's Victorian era sewers to modern Boston's state-of-the-art waste treatment facility. It is all fascinating and told with good humor and great delicacy. For more potty stories, follow up with *The Great Stink* Clare Clark's 2005 novel about the sewers and underbelly of Victorian London, and also look at *The Big Necessity: The Unmentionable World of Human Waste and Why It Matters* (2008) by Rose George for the contemporary issues of human waste disposal around the world.

Rybczynski, Witold.
Home: The Short History of an Idea. 1987. Penguin (paperback). 978-0140102314. 272pp.

> What do we mean when we say "home"? Comfort, design, privacy, and history, all play a role, and the concept as well as the structure of home has evolved over time. In this elegant essay, Rybczynski traces the Western idea of home from about 1500 to the 1980s. Rybczynski is a well-known thinker, critic, and observer of architecture and design. His work *The Perfect House: A Journey with Renaissance Master Andrea Palladio* (2003) also belongs in this list.

Sackville-West, Robert.
Inheritance: The Story of Knole and the Sackvilles. 2010. Walker and Company. 978-0802779014. 290pp.

England is an island dotted with stately homes—historic piles that serve as exemplars of architectural styles, storehouses of art and design, repositories of family skeletons, and reminders of national history. One of the oldest and grandest is Knole, home to the Sackville family since 1604. Knole isn't just a medieval mansion that became a Renaissance palace, but is also the largest private home in Britain and the repository of the Sackville family story—a family of eccentrics, royalists, and tenacious acquirers of the past. The seventh baron writes an engaging story about his family and their house.

Spawforth, Tony.
Versailles: A Biography of a Palace. 2008. St. Martin's. 978-0312357856. 320pp.

The royal chateau of Versailles takes the idea of "home" to an extravagant extreme. At different times in its history, it has been a hunting lodge, a center of government, a royal palace, a symbol of power, and to the kings and queens of 17th-century France, a home. Begun in 1623 by Louis XIII and continually expanded, it was lived in by royals, their courtiers, and battalions of servants until the French Revolution. Spawforth details the splendor and the squalor of the everyday living arrangements, which were surprisingly uncomfortable and massively complicated. Follow with Joan DeJean's *Age of Comfort: When Paris Discovered Casual and the Modern World Began* (2009).

Bright Lights, Big City—Stories of the World's Great Cities

Where people gather, cities evolve. These books look at some of the world's famous cities where history happened.

Ackroyd, Peter.
London Under: The Secret History beneath the Streets. 2011. Doubleday. 978-0385531504. 228pp.

Much goes on beneath every city—rats scurry, criminals gather, infrastructure operates, and history endures. Ackroyd, acclaimed author and biographer, is a willing explorer and thoughtful guide to the dark-and-dank underworld that still exists beneath London's streets. Ackroyd looks at the famous city from a new perspective and opens our eyes to the history beneath us all. For more London immersion, read *London: A Biography* (2001) and *Thames: The Biography* (2008) both by Peter Ackroyd or the sprawling historical fiction *London: The Novel* (1997) by Edward Rutherfurd.

De Villiers, Marq and Sheila Hirtle.
Timbuktu: The Sahara's Fabled City of Gold. 2007. Walker and Company. 978-0802714978. 302pp.

A synonym for remote, Timbuktu today is a city in the African nation of Mali where the buildings are made of mud and the unnamed streets are paved with sand. It's a city that lacks systems for sewage disposal or garbage collection. With a past cloaked in mystery and myth, it is nevertheless a place on the map of history and a rich repository of knowledge. Once known as a trading site for salt, gold, and slaves, Timbuktu was historically a center for Islamic learning and is today a World Heritage site because of its ancient mud-constructed mosques and its libraries of aging manuscripts. De Villiers and Hirtle show both the current and the historic Timbuktu.

Demetz, Peter.
Prague in Black and Gold: Scenes from the Life of a European City. 1997. Hill and Wang. 0809078430. 411pp.

Capital and largest city of the Czech Republic, Prague is an ancient city with prehistoric roots, historically a crossroads of Central European politics and cultures, and a complex place with a storied past full of learning and magic, logic and alchemy, reason and cruelty. Demetz, a child of Prague and professor of comparative literature, tells the intellectual history of the city that he loves in this comprehensive and poetic book.

Horne, Alistair.
▶ *Seven Ages of Paris.* 2002. Knopf. 978-0679454816. 480pp.

Paris, the author states, can never be boring. The city has long been a crossroads of history, a gathering place for artists, a center of power, and through it all Paris has served as a microcosm of France and the French. Horne tells the story of Paris and its people from early days as a Roman outpost on the little island felicitously situated in a calm and temperate river through expansion and construction, wars, invasions from Norsemen to Nazis, and internal upheavals brought about by kings, revolutionaries, *Communards*, and rebellious students. Horne creates a unique structure for his history, describing Paris as a woman and joyfully leading us through her seven "capriciously selected" ages. For more about the City of Lights, enjoy *Parisians: An Adventure History of Paris* (2101) by Graham Robb.

Lincoln, W. Bruce.
Sunlight at Midnight: St. Petersburg and the Rise of Modern Russia. 2000 Basic Books. 978-0465083237. 418pp.

St. Petersburg, Petrograd, Leningrad are names that express the different eras of a magnificent city. Founded by Peter the Great, construction began in 1703 on the port city that would be a "window to the West" and give Russia a gateway to the 18th-century European world of progress, invention, and

Enlightenment thinking. St. Petersburg has been home to tsars, revolutionaries, and artists, and is a city that has always contained squalor and grandeur, poverty and excessive wealth. Lincoln offers St. Petersburg as a city that can speak for the history of Russia.

Mazower, Mark.
Salonica: City of Ghosts: Christians, Muslims and Jews, 1430–1950. 2005. Knopf. 0375412980. 490pp.

> For 2,000 years, Salonica was the meeting point for the peoples, languages, cultures, and religions of the Balkan world. Greeks, Romans and Orthodox Christians, Ottomans, Byzantines and Spanish Jews, Macedonians, Muslims, and Nazis, all left an imprint on Salonica—the city that in many ways continues to thrive, yet no longer exists. Professor and historian Mazower includes many engrossing historical photographs in this fascinating portrait of a complex city.

Montefiore, Simon Sebag.
Jerusalem: The Biography. 2011. Knopf. 978-0307266514. 688pp.

> As one of the world's oldest cities and the holy gathering place for three world religions, Jerusalem throughout its history has been a center of violence and worship, massacres and messiahs, and a place where legend, history, and modernity have always mingled. Montefiore starts his story with the archaeological past and ends the main body of his book with the 1967 Six-Day War. This is a huge book covering thousands of years of history and though its scope is panoramic, it abounds with vivid detail. It is a chatty, almost gossipy, read and a grand introduction to an eternally complex city.

If You Can Make It There—New York

Chicago, Seattle, LA, and Dallas may disagree, but New York was and remains the United States' premier city. New York has long been a gathering place for people with energy, creativity, and drive. The history of New York City is varied and rich.

Carpenter, Teresa.
New York Diaries: 1609–2009. 2012. Modern Library. 978-0679643326. 512pp.

> To really be a New Yorker is to live through historic moments, to relish the peccadilloes of your compatriots, and to take it all—the history, the people, the creativity, and the cultural, intellectual, emotional, and financial life of the city—in stride. Carpenter shows New York from the intimate perspectives of the people who lived there. Diary entries from 1609 to 2009 arranged from January to December narrate the personal experience of living in this vibrant American city.

Gill, Jonathan.

Harlem: The Four Hundred Year History from Dutch Village to Capital of Black America. 2011. Grove Press. 978-0802119100. 448pp.

New York is a city comprised of exceptional neighborhoods. One of the most historic is Harlem. Author Gill looks at the geography, the events, and the personalities of Harlem as it transitioned from Native American settlement to Dutch village, from American Revolutionary hub to home for Irish, Italian, and Jewish immigrants, and to its 20th-century tenure as a center of African American culture when creative forces like Zora Neal Hurston, Langston Hughes, Duke Ellington, and Lionel Hampton called Harlem home. Dynamic writing compels you through 500 years of history of this small corner of Manhattan.

Mahler, Jonathan.

Ladies and Gentlemen, the Bronx Is Burning: 1977, Baseball, Politics, and the Battle for the Soul of a City. 2005. Farrar, Straus and Giroux. 0374175284. 356pp.

Colorful New York personalities fight for the soul of the city in parallel stories that cover baseball (Reggie Jackson's battles with manager Billy Martin) and politics (mayoral candidates Ed Koch and Mario Cuomo battling to topple incumbent mayor Beame). Meanwhile disco is battling with punk rock, the Son of Sam is randomly shooting people on the streets, and the biggest power outage the city has ever experienced is about to happen. Mahler's multilayered, crosscutting story depicts all the tension of the year when New York was a city on the brink—could it pull itself together or would it crumble into unredeemable chaos?

Nevius, Michelle and James Nevius.

Inside the Apple: A Streetwise History of New York City. 2009. Free Press. 978-1416589976. 364pp.

Like all great cities of the world, much of New York's past endures in today's streets. This narrative travel guide tells about the places where historic moments happened and where yesterday's famous New Yorkers flourished. Traces of Henry Hudson, Peter Minuit, Boss Tweed, and Elizabeth Ann Seton can yet be found in the architecture, parks, and streets of New York along with reminders of epochal American events like the Triangle factory fire, the Stonewall riots, and 9/11. The authors picked 182 locations, mostly in Manhattan, to depict interesting and memorable moments from New York's past and have written it all up in a friendly, informal style.

Okrent, Daniel.

Great Fortune: The Epic of Rockefeller Center. 2003. Viking. 978-0670031696. 544pp.

Two constants in the story of New York are money and real estate—throw in some strong personalities, art and architecture, and a sense of civic duty and you have the story of Rockefeller Center. Built in the midst of the Great

Depression, Rockefeller Center was a crowning achievement in the life of philanthropist John D. Rockefeller, Junior, son of the industrialist John D. Rockefeller, Senior. Privately funded by Junior, the original Art Deco complex of 14 buildings was derided when it opened in 1933, but quickly became a gathering place for New Yorkers and visitors from around the world. Okrent has crafted a grand book about a grand space. For another intriguing story about a famous New York building, read Stephen Birmingham's *Life at the Dakota: New York's Most Unusual Address* (1979).

Rutherfurd, Edward.
New York: The Novel. 2009. Doubleday. 978-0385521383. 880pp. FICTION

Rutherfurd's expansive novel delivers an introduction to New York's archetypal inhabitants (Native Americans, Dutch and English, African American, Irish, and Italian immigrants), big personalities, and big historic moments like Cornelius Vanderbilt, Madame Restell, the Civil War Draft Riots, and the Great Blizzard of 1888. An author in the tradition of James Michener, Rutherfurd covers almost 400 years of history by following the spreading branches of one family as it lives through history in New York City.

Shorto, Russell.
▶ *The Island at the Center of the World: The Epic Story of Dutch Manhattan and the Forgotten Colony that Shaped America.* 2004. Doubleday. 0385503490. 384pp.

Where was the idea of America formed? Many would answer in Puritan New England, but Shorto presents a case that the seat of American tolerance, individualism, insistence upon rights, and love of commerce arose in New Amsterdam—the Dutch beginnings of New York City. Focusing on the autocratic Peter Stuyvesant and the relatively unknown early patriot Adriaen van der Donck and their dealings to establish and maintain a Dutch city in the New World, Shorto shows how each brought a different ethos to the job and contributed to the creation of a uniquely American city. A witty, detailed, and fresh look at early New York.

The Watery Parts of the World— Rivers and Seas

More than being points of passage, the watery parts of the world carry culture and history. These books transport readers to the watery spaces that separate lands but connect people.

Abulafia, David.
The Great Sea: A Human History of the Mediterranean. 2011. Oxford. 978-0195323344. 816pp.

The Mediterranean is an almost landlocked extension of the Atlantic Ocean. Throughout history, it has been a trade route, a meeting place of cultures, and an arena of warfare. Egyptians, Greeks, Romans, Christians, Jews, Muslims, pirates, pilgrims, and the entire panoply of Western history have played out in the Mediterranean. Taking the story from 22,000 BC to 2010, Abulafia, a professor at Cambridge, covers every detail in this comprehensive and engrossing volume.

Hemming, John.
Tree of Rivers: The Story of the Amazon. 2008. Thames & Hudson. 978-0500514016. 368pp.

History, geography, natural science, anthropology, archaeology, and biography merge in this abundantly illustrated book about the Amazon River. Hemmings tells the Amazon's story of adventures and misadventures, of noble savages and incredible natural abundance, and of disruption by outsiders historically seeking gold, slaves, rubber, and scientific knowledge. For more about the Amazon, read *The River Sea: The Amazon in History, Myth, and Legend: A Story of Discovery* (2010) by Marshall De Bruhl.

Kaplan, Robert D.
▶ *Monsoon: The Indian Ocean and the Future of American Power.* 2010. Random House. 978-1400067466. 365pp.

Lands of the Muslim world form a ring around the Indian Ocean. Containing storied seas and famous straits (the Arabian Sea and the Straits of Hormuz) and being home to predictable winds that facilitated travel, this ocean was a highway to previous generations that enabled trade and cultural intermingling. In this series of essays about the different locations ringing the Indian Ocean, Kaplan combines travel, commentary, and history to explicate a portion of the world with a rich past and a stake in today's news.

King, Charles.
The Black Sea: A History. 2004. Oxford University Press. 978-0199241613. 304pp.

A body of water that can be foggy, stormy, and inhospitable, the Black Sea exists in a region of the world that remains unfamiliar and touches on places with historic resonance like the Balkans, Yalta, the Crimea, and the city of Odessa. The Black Sea encompasses cultures and people like the Ottomans, Greeks, and Tatars. This volume takes an academic tone to present a fascinating exploration of an exotic and little studied territory. How can you resist a book with sentences that begin "The Cossacks were precisely the kind of society that empires most worry about."

Sandlin, Lee.
Wicked River: The Mississippi When It Last Ran Wild. 2010. Pantheon. 978-0307378514. 270pp.

The importance of the Mississippi in the history and culture of America is vividly expressed by Sandlin in this engaging work that looks at the river in the 19th century before dredging, levees, locks, and dams controlled its flow.

This is a lively American history focused on the magnificent river that has been a north–south highway, locus of folklore, fiction, and myth, but also a site of danger, destruction, and joy.

Schneer, Jonathan.
The Thames. 2005. Yale. 0300107862. 330pp.

Shorter and less majestic than many of the world's famous rivers, the Thames is nevertheless "more an avenue of history than any other waterway" and a "national river in a way that other rivers are not." The Thames has been a military, economic, social, and artistic influence on English history since before history existed. From prehistory through Caesar, Magna Carta, the Blitz, to today's engineering marvel the Thames Barrier, Schneer uses tales of royalty and politicians, as well as explorations of music, poetry, and art to tell the story of England and London's past from the river that saw it all.

Centuries of Crime—Mysteries Set in the Past

The list of mysteries set in the past is huge. Undoubtedly, you have read Josephine Tey's *The Daughter of Time* and Umberto Eco's *The Name of the Rose*, and worked your way through Ellis Peters, Elizabeth Peters, and Peter Tremaine; Elliot Roosevelt, Margaret Truman, Margaret Frazer, and Lindsey Davis; Ian Pears, Robert Van Gulik, and Anne Perry; and . . . you get the idea. Well researched and often written by moonlighting experts, these stories span the world and the centuries and give readers a sense of how the world used to be.

Finch, Charles.
A Beautiful Blue Death. 2007. St Martin's Minotaur. 978-0312359775. 309pp.

Craving a detective who is a cross between Peter Wimsey and Sherlock Holmes? You will find him in Charles Lenox. All the best bits are there along with strong plots and witty prose—Victorian London in the 1860s, an aristocrat with a talent for solving crimes, a capable manservant loyal because of a traumatic event in their shared past, a close friend who is a doctor, a brother in Parliament, and sympathetic, elegant Lady Jane next door. In between murders, there is tea and toast in front of the fireplace. Follow with *The September Society* (2008), *The Fleet Street Murders* (2009), *A Stranger in Mayfair* (2010), and others.

Franklin, Ariana.
Mistress of the Art of Death. 2007. Putnam. 0399154140. 400pp.

Adelia Aquilar, possibly the 12th century's only forensic expert, is in Cambridge, England, at the request of King Henry II to solve the gruesome murders of several little children. Trained at the more liberal University of Salerno as a doctor and medical examiner, Adelia now finds herself in medieval England trying to deploy her arts while avoiding accusations of witchcraft incurred by her unusual skills. Wonderfully historical with a strong sense of setting and great story—a medieval CSI—Adelia's adventures are not for the squeamish. Her cases continue in *The Serpent's Tale* (2008), *Grave Goods* (2009), and the final book in the series *A Murderous Procession* (2010), because author Franklin passed away in 2011.

Hambly, Barbara.
Dead Water. 2004. Bantam. 978-055310964. 297pp.

Journey to 1830s New Orleans and the world of Benjamin January, a free black man with a knack for solving mysteries. This adventure takes him on a Mississippi riverboat as he searches for absconded bank funds. This is the eighth book in the series that started in 1997 with *A Free Man of Color*. *The Shirt on His Back* (2011) takes January out of his usual New Orleans milieu and to a gathering of mountain men in the Rocky Mountains. Hambly, under the name of Barbara Hamilton, also writes the Abigail Adams Mystery series that begins with *The Ninth Daughter* (2009).

Jones, J. Sydney.
The Empty Mirror: A Viennese Mystery. 2009. Minotaur Books. 0312383894. 320 pp.

Mix Conan Doyle and Caleb Carr and set them in Vienna's *Ringstrasse* and you will have a feel for J. Sydney Jones's *Empty Mirror*. Professor Hanns Gross and lawyer Karl Werther are trailblazing the field of criminology seeking answers to a series of heinous murders, victims drained of blood, and their bodies left in Vienna's famous amusement park, the *Prater*. The culture, coffee, interior design, and social conservatism of 1890s Vienna provide rich setting for this tale. Follow up with Jones's *Requiem in Vienna* (2010) or seek out Frank Tallis's Max Liebermann Mystery series for more mayhem in *fin de siècle* Vienna.

Parker, I. J.
▶ *The Convict's Sword: A Mystery of Eleventh Century Japan.* 2010. Penguin (paperback). 978-0143115793. 432pp.

Elegance, modesty, graceful manners, personal honor, and a warrior ethic permeate the society of 11th-century Tokyo, the setting for the story of Sugawara Akitada's attempt to exonerate his recently executed friend. An intriguing supporting cast, a beautiful wife, and a demanding job at the Royal Ministry of Justice where office politics and in-fighting dominate all endeavors contribute to the complicated life of the working aristocrat and sometime sleuth Akitada. Parker's excellent series begins with *The Dragon Scroll* (2005).

Pötzsch, Oliver.
The Hangman's Daughter. 2008. Mariner Books. 054774501X. 448pp.

Seldom is the executioner the most sympathetic character in a story. German author Pötzsch sets his intriguing new series featuring the Hangman and his family in Bavaria in the 1660s. The Hangman goes about his job—torture and execution—but tries to ensure that justice is observed. An unusual setting and a main character with a compassionate approach to his gruesome profession make this an absorbing historical read. Pötzsch is descended from a family of executioners, a profession with history, tradition, and an ethical stance as proud as any other.

White, Jenny.
The Sultan's Seal: A Novel. 2006. Norton. 978-0393060997. 384pp.

Istanbul, 1886, Kamil Pasha, the magistrate of Istanbul, is called upon to investigate the murder of a European woman whose jewelry connects her in some way to the sultan. American author White explores the conflicts between East and West and between modernity and tradition. The story unfolds at a leisurely pace, but White quickly establishes a strong sense of the mystery and sensuality of the declining Ottoman Empire and creates a sympathetic character in Kamil Pasha. White has two more books in the series: *The Abyssinian Proof* (2008) and *The Winter Thief* (2010). Jason Goodwin also sets his excellent mysteries in the Ottoman Empire, start with *The Janissary Tree* (2006) featuring Yashim the Eunuch.

In the Time of the Patriarchs—The World of the Old Testament

If you enjoyed Anita Diamant's 2004 best seller *The Red Tent* and Bruce Feiler's modern tour of ancient lands, *Walking the Bible* (2001), turn to these books for more exploration of the ancient Middle Eastern world and the historical backdrop for Old Testament stories and heroes.

Cahill, Thomas.
The Gifts of the Jews: How a Tribe of Desert Nomads Changed the Way Everyone Thinks and Feels (<u>Hinges of History</u>, **Book #2**). 1999. Anchor Books (paperback). 978-0385482493. 304pp.

Cahill looks at the way of thinking and the beliefs that set the ancient Jews apart from their contemporaries and allowed them to be among the founders of modern, Western thought and culture. Cahill is the author of a series of books he calls Hinges of History that look at hallmark moments in Western civilization. The series includes books about the Greeks, the Romans at the time of Christ, the medieval world, and Cahill's first best seller *How the Irish Saved Civilization* (1995), all highly recommended as thought-provoking and intriguing looks at the cultural history of mankind.

Card, Orson Scott.
Sarah (<u>Women of Genesis</u>, **Book #1**). 2000. Forge (paperback). 978-07653 41174. 352pp. FICTION

Card, best known for the young adult science fiction classic *Ender's Game* (1985), is an author of wide range and his series of books about the women of the Old Testament begins with Sarah, the formidable but aging wife of patriarch Abraham. The historical record is vague about the true existence of Abraham and Sarah, but the landscapes, customs, and behaviors Card so convincingly depicts in this story existed. Interested readers will want to follow up with *Rebekah* (2001) and *Rachel and Leah* (2004). Card's novel *Saints* is also a compelling historical novel about the beginnings of Mormonism.

Cline, Eric H.

▶ *From Eden to Exile: Unraveling Mysteries of the Bible.* 2007. National Geographic. 978-1426200847. 256pp.

Working from the perspective of archaeologist and historian Cline, a professor at the George Washington University in Washington D.C., explores the current scholarly understanding of seven "mysteries" from the Bible: the Garden of Eden, Noah's Ark, Sodom and Gomorrah, Moses and the Exodus, Joshua and the Battle of Jericho, the Ark of the Covenant, and the Ten Lost Tribes of Israel. Cline is also the author of *Biblical Archaeology: A Very Short Introduction* (2009), highly recommended for readers seeking more information about historical evidence for stories from the Bible.

Collins, Dr. Steven and Dr. Latayne C. Scott.

Discovering the City of Sodom: The Fascinating, True Account of the Discovery of the Old Testament's Most Infamous City. 2013. Simon and Schuster. 978-1451684308. 334pp.

Viewing the Bible and its stories, dates, and characters "authentically"—understanding them in terms of their original cultural context—and drawing on years as a biblical archaeologist, Collins believes he can place the ruined cities of Sodom and Gomorrah in modern Jordan at a site called Tall el-Hammam. This intriguing, somewhat controversial book offers a popular explanation of biblical excavation, detailing how to look at the finds from an ancient site. It also addresses head-on the controversies that arise when faith and history, archaeology and poetry, biography and parable converge.

Finkelstein, Israel and Neil Asher Silberman.

David and Solomon: In Search of the Bible's Sacred Kings and the Roots of the Western Tradition. 2006. Free Press (paperback). 978-0743243636. 352pp.

Legendary David—the shepherd boy who fought a giant, King of Israel, hero, lover, poet, father—and his son Solomon, a wise and just ruler who presided over a golden age in Jerusalem, are the subject of archaeological and historical investigation in this well-documented attempt to pinpoint the cultural, religious, and historic versions of the two men. Finkelstein and Silberman are sure-handed scholars who succeed in their attempt to separate "history from myth; old memoirs from later elaboration; facts from royal propaganda."

Kanner, Rebecca.
Sinners and the Sea: The Untold Story of Noah's Wife. 2013. Simon and Schuster. 978-1451695236. 339pp. FICTION

    One of the hidden women in the Bible is Noah's wife—helpmate and fellow traveler, mother of sons, and in the Bible she is never given a name. But Kanner has created a story for her as she narrates her life and the building of the Ark, the mad scramble of the doomed to survive, and the long voyage to salvation. An interesting expansion of a biblical story set in a time and place that is as much myth as history.

Rivers, Francine.
The Priest: Aaron (<u>Sons of Encouragement</u>, **Series #1**). 2004. Tyndale House. 978-0842382656. 228pp. FICTION

    In the Bible, Aaron was the brother of Moses who lived his life as a slave while Moses lived like a prince as the adopted son of the Pharaoh. But a life of bitterness turned to love and eventually Aaron became Moses's greatest supporter. Rivers offers readers a powerful portrait of the Jews in captivity and the desert life they endured in this short and engaging book that is strong on both setting and character. This is the first of five books in Rivers's <u>Sons of Encouragement</u> series that have as protagonists the lesser-known men who helped the Bible's heroes. The next book in the series is *The Warrior* (2005) about Caleb who aided Joshua.

When in Rome, or Greece, or Egypt

Are you drawn to the ancient world? Dive into these books by modern scholars with a passion for the ancient past. Each book is lively but reverent and full of information about classical Greece, Rome, and ancient Egypt.

Angela, Alberto.
▶ *A Day in the Life of Ancient Rome.* 2009. Europa. 978-1933372716. 377pp.

    From first light until midnight, author Alberto Angela guides us through a typical Roman day. Delightful and humane, this book is intelligent rather than scholarly and very entertaining. "It all begins on a Roman side street in 115 CE, during the reign of the emperor Trajan. . . . Not long before daybreak."

Beard, Mary.
The Fires of Vesuvius: Pompeii Lost and Found. 2009. Belknap/Harvard. 978-0674029767. 384pp.

    Travel with Beard through Pompeii on the horrible day in AD 79 when the great volcanic eruption froze the city in time. Beard is a classics professor at Cambridge and an excellent, witty, and erudite guide to the ancient city and the lives of its inhabitants. For more of Beard's friendly intellect, read *The Roman Triumph* (2007) or visit her blog "A Don's Life."

Hale, John R.

Lords of the Sea: The Epic Story of the Athenian Navy and the Birth of Democracy. 2009. Viking. 067002080X. 432pp.

Hale offers a new perspective on the ancient world by showing ancient Athens from the perspective of the sea—the men, ships, and engineering that conquered wherever they sailed. The Athenian warship the *trireme*, a fast-moving galley with three tiers of oars and rowers, was the basis of the navy's success. What seems like a highly esoteric and obscure topic becomes fascinating and crucial, because Hale is such an enthusiastic writer and his love for the subject comes through in every paragraph.

Haynes, Natalie.

The Ancient Guide to Modern Life. 2011. Overlook Press. 978-1590206379. 275pp.

Revisit the ancient Classics guided by someone with a light touch and a passion for the characters, events, and thinking of the ancient past. Haynes has a straightforward, authoritative voice and is friendly and funny. This is not a detailed history, but an intelligent look at the common themes of the modern and the classical worlds, like money and banking, legal systems, politics, and powerful men. Opinionated but well-reasoned, this is a fun look at the life and thought of ancient Greece and Rome—part history, part ethics, and part humor.

Mertz, Barbara.

Red Land, Black Land: Daily Life in Ancient Egypt. 2008. Harper Collins. 978-0061252747. 410pp.

In this revised and updated edition of her 1966 overview of the people of ancient Egypt, Mertz offers an easy-flowing look at life in the Black Land, the fertile strips of land along the Nile, and the Red Land, the dry and hostile deserts just beyond. Mertz is a lively guide—justifiably opinionated, casually chatty, and unquestionably well informed. This is an outstanding, general introduction to a complex and eternally fascinating culture. Under the name Elizabeth Peters, Barbara Mertz is the author of the Amelia Peabody Mystery series set in Egypt, starting with *Crocodile on the Sandbank* (1975).

Perrottet, Tony.

The Naked Olympics: The True Story of the Ancient Games. 2004. Random House. 978-0812969917. 240pp. ⓎⒶ

Held every four years from 776 BC to AD 394—a 1,200-year run without interruption or cancellation—the ancient Olympic Games were about more than sports, they combined all aspects of life, ceremony, and celebration. The competitions were often glorious and the conditions for the spectators were always rigorous—intense heat, inadequate available water, minimal lodging, and a remote location. Perrottet likens the experience to attending a badly planned rock concert. Entertaining, humorous, and insightful, this is a unique look at the classical world of ancient Greece through its most all-encompassing recurring spectacle.

Rosen, William.
Justinian's Flea: The First Great Plague and the End of the Roman Empire.
2007. Viking. 978-0670038558. 367pp.

The Roman Empire continued in the east after Rome fell in the West. But, in 542, plague arrived in Constantinople—the current capitol of the empire. As the empire's citizens sickened and died, Europe—also home to expanding populations of Goths, Franks, Huns, Muslims, and Slavs—was remade. Rosen covers broad territory in this story of the marvelous city of Constantinople, the Emperor Justinian, his illustrious wife, generals and contemporaries, and the disease that aided the demise of the classical world of Late Antiquity and the birth of medieval Europe.

Chapter Four

Language

Sometimes, it is the way a book is written that offers the most appeal for a reader. Form and style, length and pacing, all contribute to the language appeal of a work.

The following lists offer a variety of narrative styles from the serendipitous experience of reading traditional reference books to the "you are there" feeling created by eyewitness accounts to the elegant fusion of words and pictures in graphic novels. You will find tomes of depth and detail, because some readers want to be enveloped in an event, an era, or a life and seek out works to satisfy that desire for immersion. On the opposite end of the length spectrum are readers who love short, snappy, get-to-the-point kinds of books and you will also find these concise read-it-and-move-on volumes in the following lists. Unusual uses of language and narrative structures that challenge readers' expectations also figure in this chapter of history books with language appeal.

The Story of a Book

People who love to read often love to read books about books. The making, preserving, and meaning of books are grand topics for bibliophiles. These works focus on the enduring power of books as objects and as carriers of ideas.

Bakewell, Sarah.
How to Live: Or a Life of Montaigne in One Question and Twenty Attempts at an Answer. 2010. Other Press. 978-1590514252. 400pp. 🕮

French nobleman Michel de Montaigne (1533–1592) retired to his estates in 1571 to read his books (his library was vast for the day), to think, and write about his life. The essays that were the products of his years of contemplation offered a mix of personal history, topical anecdote, philosophical musings, and timeless observation. With his writing, Montaigne created a model for the personal essay that writers have emulated through the centuries. In her unique and captivating book, Bakewell explores different aspects of Montaigne's life and thought bringing the man, his writings, and the French Renaissance to vibrant life.

Lansky, Aaron.

▶ *Outwitting History: The Amazing Adventures of a Man Who Rescued a Million Yiddish Books.* 2004. Algonquin. 978-1565124295. 328pp.

As a graduate student, Aaron Lansky found his passion: rescuing the fast-disappearing world of Yiddish books. Treks to the musty apartments of elderly Jews and midnight missions to search through dumpsters led to the salvation of a million books and the creation of the Yiddish Book Center in Amherst, Massachusetts. Lansky tells a spirited story about a treasure trove that no one considered to be treasure, and a young man on a mission that turned a nerdy endeavor into a heroic quest. Adina Hoffman and Peter Cole tell another story of lost texts recovered in *Sacred Trash: The Lost and Found World of the Cairo Geniza* (2011).

Nicholson, Adam.

God's Secretaries: The Making of the King James Bible. 2003. Harper. 978-0060185169. 281pp.

James I took the throne of England in 1603 and almost immediately set a colossal task for scholars of his realm—translate the Bible into a form that would reflect contemporary sensibilities and provide English churches with an authorized version. To create a work of textual clarity and poetic richness, the translators, a group of almost 50 men—well-known to each other but little known to us today—employed simple vocabulary, rhythmic prose, and an overall majestic tone. Their seven years of labor was a successful undertaking that created a hallmark of English prose and a memorial to James I, the king who created the committee that translated the Bible.

Rehak, Melanie.

Girl Sleuth: Nancy Drew and the Women Who Created Her. 2005. Harcourt. 0151010412. 364pp.

The creation and evolution of Nancy Drew, a girl detective and American icon, is detailed in this behind-the-scenes look. The Stratemeyer publishing syndicate was responsible for the Hardy Boys and the Bobbsey Twins and in 1930 introduced Nancy Drew. The author of the books was listed as Carolyn Keene, but really was Stratemeyer's daughter Harriet, lively journalist Mildred

Benson, as well as other women and several men who wrote to a formula and swore to maintain the confidentiality of their authorship. An interesting look at publishing, mid-century American working women, and one of America's enduring cultural icons clever, brave near perfect Nancy Drew.

Reynolds, David S.
Mightier than the Sword: Uncle Tom's Cabin and the Battle for America. 2011. Norton. 978-0393081329. 351pp.

Uncle Tom's Cabin was a popular sensation from the moment of its publication in 1852. It became the 19th century's biggest best seller after the Bible. Reynolds set out to write the biography of this book and to show its impact on history. Did the book cause the Civil War? Did the film versions perpetuate Jim Crow? Why was Uncle Tom, a strong and noble character in the novel, transformed by popular culture into a weak, simpering, racial sellout? Stowe's enduring novel with its reputation for hackneyed sentimentality and stereotypical characters is newly explored by Reynolds and presented as an emotion rich product of its times filled with action and adventure that is equally about relationships, tolerance, gender, law, religion, family, and democracy—a book, Reynolds argues, that remains a cultural force for good.

Ryback, Timothy W.
Hitler's Private Library: The Books That Shaped His Life. 2008. Knopf. 978-1400042043. 304pp.

Can we understand the mind of a man by looking at the books he owns? Ryback poses this question as he looks at a selection of volumes owned, read, and presumably scribbled in by Adolf Hitler. Hitler was an autodidact and a voracious reader who was a grateful recipient of books—books being a reliably safe gift to bestow upon der Fuhrer. At one time, he had a large and eclectic book collection. The books were scattered after the war, but the Library of Congress now houses 1,200 and others languish in archives and libraries and probably in private attics and cellars around the world. Ryback uses some of Hitler's books to look at different moments and themes in the life of one of history's most impenetrable figures.

Soskice, Janet.
The Sisters of Sinai: How Two Lady Adventurers Discovered the Hidden Gospels. 2009. Knopf. 978-1400041336. 316pp.

Scottish twin sisters born in 1843 become unlikely lady adventurers when they set out on a quest to the Middle East seeking ancient biblical manuscripts. Along the way, they become world-class scholars and intrepid travelers. But treachery awaits them—and not on caravan with the Bedouins in the Sinai desert, but back at Cambridge among the civilized but cutthroat university-trained scholars! A fast-paced, exciting read about two strong-willed women who believed in themselves and their mission.

We Were There—Eyewitness Histories

Letters, diaries, and eyewitness accounts tell us history as it happened. These volumes make history an intimate, almost private affair, giving readers access to moments not filtered, selected, and arranged by historians, but reported by someone who was there.

Blanc, Olivier.
Last Letters: Prisons and Prisoners of the French Revolution. 1989. FSG. 978-0374521882. 250pp.

> These poignant letters from French citizens—aristocrats, artisans, shopkeepers, and a queen—were written from prison on the eve of each authors' execution at the hands of the revolutionaries. The letters tell of universal themes that transcended the moment of terror—love of family, concern for the future of children, pleasure in the simple joys that life offered, and regret. Were these people active enemies of the state or victims caught up in the increasing frenzy of the Reign of Terror? Found bundled in a French bureaucratic archive, the letters had never been sent to their intended recipients.

Carey, John, editor.
Eyewitness to History. 1989. Harvard (paperback). 0380729687. 706pp.

> Oxford professor John Carey compiled over 300 eyewitness accounts describing major events and small personal moments that show the world and the activities of people over the last 24 centuries. Drawing from diaries, letters, travel books, autobiographies, and memoirs, each account is a brief moment of time travel—a subjective, unmediated expression of an experience from the past narrated by someone who was there. This is an older volume that will never seem dated, and it leaves readers with deep feeling for the humanity in the history. David Colbert's *Eyewitness to America: 500 Years of American History in the Words of Those Who Saw It Happen* (1998) offers a similar exploration of firsthand accounts of American history.

Grunwald, Lisa and Stephen J. Adler, editors.
Letters of the Century: America 1900–1999. 1999. Dial. 978-0385315906. 740pp.

> Famous, infamous, and unknown correspondents narrate significant moments of 20th-century America in this eclectic volume of 400 letters. Events that dominated the world stage, like President Truman's terse authorization to drop the atomic bomb on Hiroshima, and events that were private and small, like Mickey Mantle's encouraging epistle to a young polio victim, are equally engrossing when told through the words of people who were there. Also of interest by Lisa Grunwald *Women's Letters: America from the Revolutionary War to the Present* (2005).

Kennedy, Caroline and Michael Bechloss.
Jacqueline Kennedy: Historic Conversations on Life with John F. Kennedy.
2011. Hyperion. 978-1401324254. 400pp.

A very private woman with a deep sense of obligation to posterity, Jacqueline Kennedy sat with historian and author Arthur M. Schlesinger in early 1964 just months after the assassination of her husband and recorded her memories of their lives together. The transcripts were locked away and left to the future. Her surviving daughter, Caroline Kennedy decided to publish them as part of the commemoration of the 50th anniversary of John F. Kennedy's presidency. Mrs. Kennedy's strong personality and insightful intelligence come through as she muses about her time in the White House, her husband's personality, their private and political life, world leaders, historic moments, and her husband's possible legacy. The book is fascinating, and the audiotapes that accompany it are equally intriguing.

Koppel, Lily.
Red Leather Diary: Reclaiming a Life through the Pages of a Lost Journal.
2008. Harper. 978-0061256776. 336pp.

Journalist Koppel uncovered a little slice of personal history in a pile of old trunks being cleaned out of a New York basement. The discovery of a teenager's diary from the 1920s and 1930s started the reporter's odyssey to find the author, Florence Wolfson. Unlike diarists like Anne Frank, Samuel Pepys, Victor Klemperer, or Mary Chestnut, Wolfson commented only little on the momentous events of her times. Instead, she expressed the joy and anxieties of a lively girl growing up in a vibrant city at a certain moment. Koppel's story of the diary, the teenager, and the woman she became makes for an engaging read about how we craft and record our lives.

Mallon, Thomas.
▶ *A Book of One's Own: People and Their Diaries.* 1984. Ticknor and Fields. 978-0899192420. 318pp.

Throughout time and across the globe, people have confided their thoughts and the events of their lives to diaries. Mallon organizes well-known (like Virginia Woolf, Albert Speer, Anais Nin, etc.) and little-known diarists into like-minded groups—chroniclers, travelers, pilgrims, creators, confessors, prisoners, etc. He showcases the writers' personalities and the power and subtlety of the diary genre through his clever choice of excerpts and anecdotes and his own witty analysis and commentary. Although Mallon's book is out of print, it is available from many libraries and used book sellers.

A Picture Is Worth a Thousand Words— Graphic History

Two acknowledged history classics in graphic novel form are Marjane Satrapi's *Persepolis: The Story of a Childhood* (2007) and Art Spiegelman's *The*

Complete Maus: A Survivor's Tale (1996). But other artist/authors have taken up the challenge and created works that blend pictures and words to transport readers to another time and a greater understanding of the past. The books in this list offer a sampling of artists and authors telling history in a slightly different way.

Abadzis, Nick.
▶ *Laika.* 2007. Turtleback. 978-1417779321. 204pp. Ⓨ🄰
    In November 1957, Russia launched Sputnik 2, a satellite that would orbit the earth. Onboard was Laika, a little stray mutt who had been found on the streets of Moscow and trained for space flight. Abadzis tells Laika's story using many facts and some fiction. He creates a graphic novel true to the history and with all the pathos you expect in a dog story.

Doxiadis, Apostolos and Christos H. Papadimitriou. Illustrated by Alecos Papadatos and Annie Di Donna.
Logicomix: An Epic Search for Truth. 2009. Bloomsbury. 978-1596914520. 352pp.
    Bertrand Russell (1872–1970)—philosopher, logician, pacifist, and social critic—engaged in a lifelong search to find the truth behind mathematics and therefore, he believed, the truth behind life. His journey to knowledge was often tortured and wrought with intellectual drama. Doxiadis makes the turmoil of Russell's life very apparent in his drawings and choice of episodes. Biography is a vibrant area in graphic novel publishing; for more biographies, try Rick Geary's works on Trotsky and J. Edgar Hoover, *The 14th Dalai Lama* (2010) by Tetsu Saiwai, or *Che: A Graphic Biography* (2008) by Spain Rodriquez.

Fink, Sam.
The Declaration of Independence: The Words That Made America. 2002. Scholastic. 0439407001. 160pp. Ⓨ🄰
    The text of the Declaration of Independence hand lettered and illustrated to bring out the full meaning and importance of the document. Includes a chronology, a glossary and a list of resources. This is a book that brings words on a piece of paper to vibrant life and makes you think about each phrase in the document that started America.

Gopnick, Adam.
A Cartoon History of the Modern World Part 1: From Columbus to the Constitution. 2006. Collins Reference. 978-0060760045. 272pp. Ⓨ🄰
    Exuberant and informative, Gopnick has a winning combination of visuals and slightly irreverent but well-informed text. His view of history is international and he includes intellectual movements as well as wars and social history along with explorations and politics. Gopnick also provides a nice bibliography and an index. Follow up with *A Cartoon History of the Modern*

World Part 2: From the Bastille to Baghdad (2009) or with Gopnick's prequels the multivolume *Cartoon History of the Universe.*

Hennessey, Jonathan and Aaron McConnell.
The United States Constitution: A Graphic Adaptation. 2008. Hill and Wang. 978-0809094875. 160pp. ⊻Ⓐ

If you are looking for a refresher course on the Constitution, this informative graphic novel is the ticket. Each article and amendment is explained. Earnest and straightforward, this is a great introduction or a good reminder of the lasting power of the U.S. Constitution.

Jacobsen, Sid and Ernie Colon.
The 9/11 Report: A Graphic Adaptation. 2006. Hill and Wang. 0809057395. 144pp.

The *9/11 Commission Report* is translated into a dramatic graphic retelling in this powerful work. The authors stated their goal as creating a greater understanding of what happened on that day in history. Jacobsen and Colon want to share the story with as many people as possible, arguing that a well-informed public with an awareness of events and their meaning contributes to the security of a nation.

Pekar, Harvey and Paul Buhle.
Studs Terkel's Working: A Graphic Adaptation. 2009. New Press. 978-1595583215. 208pp.

Showcasing the work of multiple artists, this graphic work illustrates excerpts from Terkel's 1974 oral history classic *Working: People Talk About What They Do All Day and How They Feel About What They Do.* Studs Terkel was renowned for his oral histories and had a long career as a writer, a Chicago radio personality, and an interviewer of regular folk. His other well-known works are the Pulitzer Prize–winning *The Good War: An Oral History of World War II* (1984) and *Hard Times: An Oral History of the Great Depression* (1970).

Redniss, Lauren.
Radioactive: Marie and Pierre Curie: A Tale of Love and Fallout. 2010. It Books. 978-0061351327. 208pp.

Not quite a graphic novel, but not a traditional text either. Redniss uses drawings, collage, photographs, and words to tell the story of the relationship between Marie and Pierre Curie and their scientific explorations. The result is an unusual and alluring reading experience. For another fascinating look at history through art, seek out David King's *Red Star over Russia: A Visual History of the Soviet Union from the Revolution to the Death of Stalin* (2009).

Sacco, Joe. ♆
Palestine: The Special Edition. 2007. Fantagraphic Books. 978-560978442. 285pp.

Readers who think graphic novels are just long comics will understand their power after reading *Palestine*. Sacco delivers a sobering and sometimes brutal retelling of his attempts to understand the Israeli–Palestinian conflict through his travels to the area and meetings with citizens there. This edition compiles the nine "comic books" where this material was originally published and includes an introduction by Edward Said and an essay by Sacco where he discusses his intellectual and creative process.

Often Quoted, Always Remembered— American Texts That Still Have Impact

In the story of any nation, there are words, speeches, and texts that helped create the national ethos. These books look at the words that shaped America and still have impact for us today.

Boritt, Gabor.
The Gettysburg Gospel: The Lincoln Speech That Nobody Knows. 2006. Simon and Schuster. 978-0743288200. 415pp.

At Gettysburg in November 1863 just months after the horrendously bloody battle, President Lincoln gave a speech lasting barely two minutes, yet his remarks became an enduring reaffirmation of democracy and one of America's most famous speeches. In this meticulous work of history and analysis, Boritt reconstructs the event and deconstructs the speech. Summarizing the appeal of the speech, Boritt states: "The world's love of Lincoln's address focuses on the beauty of its language, its devotion to democracy, and above all its eternal promise of 'a new birth of freedom' for all 'the people.'"

Hansen, Drew.
The Dream: Martin Luther King, Jr. and the Speech That Inspired a Nation. 2003. HarperCollins. 0060084766. 293pp.

On a hot day in late August 1963, an estimated quarter million people assembled in Washington D.C. to march for civil rights. They gathered peacefully at the Washington Monument and walked quietly to the Lincoln Memorial for a program of entertainment and speeches. The Reverend Dr. Martin Luther King Jr. spoke late in the program and his stirring oration remains in our national memory as a civil rights landmark. Using biblical resonance, patriotic imagery, and the "soaring refrains of hope" that brought the speech to its rousing conclusion, King inspired the nation. Hansen analyses the text, the delivery, and the reception of the speech that put King on the national stage and helped advanced the rights of all Americans.

Jones, Jeffrey Owen and Peter Meyer.
The Pledge: A History of the Pledge of Allegiance. 2010. Thomas Dunne. 978-0312350024. 224pp.

The Pledge of Allegiance, one brief sentence, is probably the most spoken piece of prose in America—new citizens, school children, Scouts, Elks and legislators recite it regularly and with pride. Contrary to sentimental mythologizing, George Washington and Benjamin Franklin never said it. The Pledge of Allegiance was written in 1892 and originally published in a children's magazine; Congress adopted it in 1942. Oddly enough, that little sentence meant to express love of country and adherence to a national ideal has long been a political and cultural hot potato—controversy, contention, and disagreement have dogged it from the start. Jones and Meyer share the interesting history and ongoing controversies surrounding the Pledge of Allegiance.

Kennedy, Caroline.
▶ *The Patriot's Handbook: Songs, Poems, Stories, and Speeches Celebrating the Land We Love.* 2003. Hyperion. 978-0786869183. 688pp. ⓎⒶ
An eclectic anthology of words that have defined, expressed, and shaped America. Kennedy invokes history, emotion, and controversy in her selections of presidential speeches, song lyrics, excerpts from novels, judicial opinions, poems, and photographs. Stating that "patriotism requires understanding," Kennedy hopes readers will use this collection as a starting place for their own explorations of the rights, responsibilities, and joys of being an American.

Meyerson, Michael.
Liberty's Blueprint: How Madison and Hamilton Wrote the Federalist Papers, Defined the Constitution, and Made Democracy Safe for the World. 2008. Basic Books. 978-0465002641. 309pp.
The Federalist is a series of essays written in 1777 and 1778 by James Madison, Alexander Hamilton, and John Jay (though he contributed to only a few essays). The essays were written as propaganda to convince the men of the day to ratify the Constitution. Hamilton and Madison, writing under a pseudonym, crafted 85 essays in an attempt to sell a new form of government and a new way of thinking about politics and civic life. Meyerson, a teacher of constitutional law, offers explication of the essays. He also writes about the relationship of these two men, both brilliant and sincere, but with very different styles and personalities: priggish Madison, volatile Hamilton.

Monk, Linda.
The Words We Live By: Your Annotated Guide to the Constitution. 2003. Hyperion. 0786867205. 288pp. ⓎⒶ
Using contemporary examples and historical context, Monk explicates the entire U.S. Constitution and each amendment by parsing the document phrase by phrase and explaining what every bit of it means. Monk uses sidebars, illustrations, and quotations to explain the arcane original language and the deeper, often disputed meanings of our national document. Truly aimed at the general reader who wants a better understanding of the Constitution, this is a great resource for teens and new citizens. For another deep examination of the Constitution, read Akhil Reed Amar's *America's Constitution: A Biography* (2005).

Witham, Larry.
A City Upon a Hill: How Sermons Changed the Course of American History.
2007. HarperCollins. 0060854278. 336pp.

> From small congregations to huge camp meetings, right up to radio and television broadcasts, preaching in America has been a way to transmit ideas and influence the people. Witham, a prize-winning journalist, looks at the flow of American history through the personalities of the men and women whose preaching reached the nation. He analyses the rhetoric they employed and the larger social movements they preached about—Prohibition, abolition, civil rights, women's suffrage, wars, and peace. Drawing on Catholic, Protestant, and Jewish traditions and showing both the good and the questionable, this is a fast-flowing narrative that looks at American history and thought from an interesting, underused perspective.

Long Ago for Short Attention Spans— History under 300 Pages

Sometimes, you want a quick read to give you the general outlines of a topic. This is an eclectic mix of titles and topics and each book tackles a vast subject in fewer than 300 pages. Each of these titles will leave you well informed but still young.

Armstrong, Karen.
Islam: A Short History. 2002. Modern Library. 978-0812966183. 272pp.

> Armstrong lucidly summarizes the founding, evolution, and expansion of Islam, giving an overview of the complex relationships and familial quarrels and exploring the enduring tension between fundamentalism and moderation, and the historic and contemporary interplay of the traditional Muslim world and the modern West. British author Armstrong is an expert on the history of religion and comparative religion, among her other recommended works are *A History of God: The 4,000 Year Quest of Judaism, Christianity and Islam* (1993), *A Short History of Myth* (2006), and *Buddha* (2004)

Gonzalez-Crussi, Frank.
▶ *A Short History of Medicine.* 2007. Modern Library. 978-0679643432. 272pp.

> The history of medicine is the story of the slow accumulation of knowledge. Retired professor of pathology Gonzalez-Crussi considers the evolution of different medical fields—anatomy, surgery, anesthesia, reproduction, disease, and diagnosis—and presents some of the diverse thinking and personalities who confronted scientific mysteries and defied religious, social, and cultural taboos to gradually expose truth and create understanding. This book is a survey course written for generalists that offers an elegant context for

understanding humanity's continuing quest to alleviate suffering, advance health, battle disease, and challenge death.

Horne, Alistair.
The Age of Napoleon. 2004. Modern Library. 978-0679642633. 240pp.

In his introduction, Horne mentions there are over 600,000 books with Napoleon as their subject; this book is a nice one to start with. Horne looks at Napoleon's times and years of influence in France from 1795 to 1820. Horne includes only the barest mention of battles, but instead emphasizes social milieu and includes interesting tidbits about dress styles, the theater, architecture, and the grand personalities, colleagues, enemies, and lovers that surrounded Napoleon and helped create an age.

Johnson, Paul.
Churchill. 2009. Viking. 978-0670021055. 192pp.

Can the long and eventful life of one of the huge personalities of the 20th century be summed up in less than 200 pages? The answer is a resounding yes. This excellent introduction written by the prolific, opinionated Johnson hits the highlights and gives a comprehensive view of the energy of the young Churchill, the steadfast commitment of the elder statesman, and the lifelong eccentricities of the man. Ex-journalist Johnson admitted he had to be ruthless in writing such a short book and hoped that readers would move on to learn more about Churchill and particularly to read Churchill's own writings.

Lord, Walter.
A Night to Remember: The Classic Account of the Final Hours of the Titanic. 2004 (originally published in 1955). Holt Paperbacks. 978-0805077643. 182pp. ⓎⒶ

In succinct and compelling prose, Lord details almost minute by minute the sinking of the great ship, the scramble to the lifeboats, the heroism, and then the stunned acceptance of the greatest sea disaster to date. Sixty-three survivors still alive in 1955 contributed to Lord's chronicle recounting their memories—not just of facts, but also of feelings and atmosphere, the joy of being a passenger on the magnificent ship, and the terror of being a survivor. Though his book is short, it is full of tension, suspense, humanity, and pathos—a very emotional book.

Rybczynski, Witold.
One Good Turn: A Natural History of the Screwdriver and the Screw. 2001. Scribner. 978-0002000314. 176pp.

Tools and toolmaking are themes that predate recorded history. In this very brief book on a very small topic, Rybczynski examines the history of the *turnscrew*, as the screwdriver was once called, and the screw. Carpentry, weaponry, printing, and art, all have been impacted by the simple helix shape of the screw. Rybczynski is an elegant, articulate writer who offers absorbing, philosophically inclined books about design, architecture, and place. For another intriguing look at the history and design of an essential tool, read *The Pencil* (1992) by Henry Petroski.

Bite-Sized History—Every Chapter a New Story

Pithy and to the point, these books offer no fuss, no muss stories from the past in bite-sized chunks. These books are especially recommended for young readers and readers who like a lighter approach.

Beyer, Rick.
The Greatest Stories Never Told: 100 Tales from History to Astonish, Bewilder, and Stupefy. 2003. Harper. 978-0060014018. 224pp. ⓎⒶ

Fun and friendly, these tidbits of history were originally written for *Timeline 2000*, a series that aired on the History Channel during the millennium year. Brief historical teasers with nice illustrations and reliable sources make this a solid work with a light presentation; it is great for just dipping into. Would it surprise you to learn that Attila the Hun died of a bloody nose, that the letters on the first typewriter keyboards were arranged to slow typists down, or that modesty was the real reason behind the invention of the stethoscope? A self-described history buff and lifelong student of history, Beyer, a documentary filmmaker, went on to create a whole series of books, and fans of this volume will also want to read *The Greatest War Stories Never Told* (2005).

Chaline, Eric.
Fifty Animals That Changed the Course of History. 2011. Firefly. 978-1554078974. 223pp. ⓎⒶ

The cat, the dog, the pig, and the horse are to be expected—but the leech, the cod, the falcon, and the bat? Chaline makes good arguments for all 50 of the animals he includes in this lovely book about the intersection of natural history and human civilization. Not all the relationships have been benign—sometimes humans have suffered, more often animals bear the brunt of mankind's ambition—but as Chaline shows, "without animals, human history would be much poorer." This is an elegant book with many illustrations.

Davis, Kenneth C.
▶ *Don't Know Much About History, Anniversary Edition: Everything You Need to Know About American History but Never Learned.* 2011. Harper. 978-0061960536. 752pp. ⓎⒶ

This fun read covers lots of history in brief, spirited segments. Arranged chronologically, Davis provides background and offers answers to recurring historical questions, like "What was the Lost Colony?" "Who were the suffragists?"

"What did Lincoln and Douglas debate?" "What happened in Watts?" Nicely documented with an annotated bibliography of selected sources, Davis filled a reader's void with the entire <u>Don't Know Much</u> series of best-selling books that offer short and snappy explanations of large topics like history, geography, mythology, the Bible, and the Civil War.

Flude, Kevin.
Divorced, Beheaded, Died: The History of Britain's Kings and Queens in Bite-sized Chunks. 2010. Michael O'Mara. 184317362X. 176pp.

British royalty always makes for interesting reading—they ruled empires, waged wars, advanced culture, changed history, but in some ways, were just regular folks with a lot of family issues. Volumes exist about each family member, but Flude's small book offers a few lines or a few pages about each king and queen, giving only the most salient facts about all of England's rulers—legendary figures, Roman generals, and Oliver Cromwell included. This is an enjoyable and concise introduction to a topic that could become a lifetime reading plan. Flude's bibliography is also brief and lists some very current, approachable books.

Lee, Laura.
Blame It on the Rain: How the Weather Has Changed History. 2006. Harper (paperback). 0060839821. 336pp. 🅨🅐

For much of man's existence, attention to the weather could mean the difference between survival and death like knowing when to plant crops to ensure the best harvest, or to avoid the ocean when seething weather-whipped waves might take a ship to the bottom of the sea. In this breezy book, Lee addresses the weather and each chapter tells the complete story of an historical moment when the weather determined the outcome. Did Robespierre fall because rain dispersed his final supporters? Was the Little Ice Age responsible for the mellifluous sound of Stradivari's instruments? Throughout history, has Russia's secret weapon really been winter? Speculative and thought-provoking essays make you reconsider great men and historic moments in the context of the wind, rain, and snow.

Martin, Paul.
Secret Heroes: Everyday Americans Who Shaped Our World. 2012. William Morrow (paperback). 978-0062096043. 352pp. 🅨🅐

In sprightly, brief biographies, Martin tells about the lives of 30 Americans who don't get the attention of a George Washington or an Eleanor Roosevelt—people like Ishi, the last living member of his California Native American tribe; Eliza Scidmore, the woman who beautified Washington D.C. by importing cherry trees from Japan; Clarence Saunders, the man who gave us Piggly Wiggly and the first self-serve grocery stores; and Hugh Thompson, the soldier who intervened in the My Lai massacre saving Vietnamese civilians and exhibiting the greatest "ethical wartime behavior."

Sandler, Martin.
Lost to Time: Unforgettable Stories That History Forgot. 2010. Sterling. 978-1402729584. 289pp.

    Eleven stories of people and events that you probably never heard of, like the 1871 Peshtigo forest fire, a deadlier conflagration than the Chicago fire that happened on the same day; and Gil Eanes, the little acknowledged adventurer who pushed the boundaries of the known world for Henry II of Portugal by rounding the terrifying Cape Bojador on the coast of Africa and discovering that the world did not end on the other side. Sandler's brisk prose and apt selection makes discovering these little-known moments of history a treat.

History's Tomes—Huge Books with Depth and Detail

Why do people say "Tome" as if it were a bad thing? Sometimes, you want overwhelming amounts of evidence, a diversity of personalities, multiple story lines, depth, and detail. These doorstoppers provide scholarly narratives for those times when you want a long, involved look at a topic. The subjects are diverse. The only thing these books have in common is heft.

Figes, Orlando.
▶ *Natasha's Dance: A Cultural History of Russia.* 2003. Picador. 978-0312421953. 768pp.

    The cultural life of any nation is vast and multilayered. Figes takes a thematic look at Russian culture with the goal of discovering a Russian identity. His exploration begins with the building of St. Petersburg and ends in the 1960s having touched on film and music, dance and design, poetry, prose, and much of the "mental bric-a-brac that constitute a culture and a way of life." This is an absorbing, leisurely investigation of how artists have both observed and created the concept of Russia.

MacMillan, Margaret.
Paris 1919: Six Months That Changed the World. 2002. Random House. 978-0375508264. 570pp.

    With thorough scholarship and appropriate bits of gossip thrown in, MacMillan shows us the year when many of the world's current troubles began. She vividly portrays the personalities in charge of recreating the map of the world following World War I while inadvertently creating the foundations of future turmoil in the Balkans, the Middle East, and the Soviet Union, and creating the underpinnings of World War II.

Royle, Trevor.
The British Civil War: The Wars of the Three Kingdoms, 1638–1660. 2004. Palgrave. 0312292937. 888pp.

This massive work is largely military history about the British Civil War—a series of battles, power struggles, and political, religious, and social upheavals that took place across England, Scotland, and Ireland in the 1600s. But Royle includes so many colorful characters and human moments that his story becomes a rousing overview of Britain in a time of tumult and change. Perhaps, because he relied on the accounts of many diarists and letter writers, Royle creates an intimate story of the national drama of Cavaliers and Roundheads, Charles I, Cromwell, Charles II, and others. This is a leisurely armchair read. Royle has also written acclaimed books about that other complex British family squabble, the War of the Roses, as well as books about the Crimean War, Field Marshall Montgomery, and Kitchener.

Strassler, Robert B., editor.
The Landmark Herodotus: The Histories. 2007. Anchor Books (paperback). 978-1400031146. 953pp.

You remember Herodotus—ancient Greek, Father of History. Strasser has taken this classic and created an edition that supports all aspect of Herodotus's text—essays in the appendix written by prominent classicists give insight to the times, headers and marginal synopses on every page help keep you in the game, and an excellent index, multiple maps, helpful footnotes, and a new translation create greater understanding and deeper involvement with this seminal historical text. This is a truly great reading experience. To enjoy another tome of equal stature, move on to Strassler's *Landmark Thucydides.*

Tomsen, Peter.
The Wars of Afghanistan: Messianic Terrorism, Tribal Conflicts, and the Failures of Great Powers. 2011. Public Affairs. 978-1586487638. 912pp.

With firsthand knowledge of the contemporary situation and deep cultural and historical understanding of the region, Tomsen, a former American diplomat, tells the complex story of Afghanistan—a country based upon tribe, clan, and kin that has resisted central authority and outside interference for thousands of years. Tomsen rapidly takes the story from Alexander the Great to the post-9/11 reality, focusing most of his writing on the last 30 years. Tomsen's deep compassion, acute intelligence, and expert knowledge inform every page. He has done a public service in writing this book and offering a context for understanding Afghanistan. For more on the topic, read *Ghost Wars: The Secret History of the CIA, Afghanistan, and Bin Laden, from the Soviet Invasion to September 10, 2001* (2004) by Steve Coll.

Scribble, Scribble, Eh Mr. Gibbon— Multivolume Sets

When Gibbon presented the latest volume of *The Decline and Fall of the Roman Empire* to the Duke of Gloucester the, unbookish royal famously said, "Another big fat book—scribble, scribble, eh Mr. Gibbon?" The duke may have declined to be enthralled by sheer size, but many readers love the challenge of length and depth. Each of these multivolume masterpieces offers you a long-term commitment to an author and set of ideas—your reward—great writing, a comprehensive view, and many hours immersed in the past.

Atkinson, Rick. The Liberation Trilogy.
An Army at Dawn: The War in North Africa, 1942–1943. 2002. Henry Holt and Co. 978-0805062885. 681pp.
The Day of Battle: The War in Sicily and Italy, 1943–1944. 2007. Henry Holt and Co. 978-0805062892. 791pp.
The Guns at Last Light: The War in Western Europe, 1944–1945. 2013. Henry Holt and Co. 978-0805062908. 896pp.

    Atkinson narrates the momentous story of the American military role in the defeat of the Nazi's and the liberation of Europe during World War II. Journalist and Army brat, Atkinson received the 2010 Pritzker Prize for lifetime achievement in military history writing. His 1989 book *The Long Gray Line* about West Point and the generation of graduates who fought in Vietnam is a classic.

Boorstin, Daniel. The Americans.
The Colonial Experience. 1958. Vintage (paperback). 978-0394705132. 448pp.
The National Experience. 1965. Vintage (paperback). 978-0394703589. 528pp.
The Democratic Experience. 1973. Vintage (paperback). 978-0394710112. 736pp.

    Still in print and available after many years, Boorstin's famous trilogy immerses readers in a lively and entertaining exploration of the moments, people, and thinking that shaped America. Historian, professor, and Librarian of Congress, Daniel Boorstin wrote amiable and articulate books about history and even his bibliographic notes make delightful and intriguing reading. Boorstin's later trilogy comprised of international stories about humanity's ongoing intellectual strivings is also highly recommended: *The Discoverers* (1982), *The Creators* (1992), and *The Seekers* (1998).

Branch, Taylor. America in the King Years.
Parting the Waters: America in the King Years, 1954–63. 1988. Simon & Schuster. 978-0671460976. 1,088pp.
Pillar of Fire: America in the King Years, 1963–65. 1998. Simon & Schuster. 978-0684808192. 768pp.
At Canaan's Edge: America in the King Years, 1965–68. 2006. Simon & Schuster. 978-0684857121. 1,056pp.

    Calling this work a "wondrous obsession," Branch meant to spend 3 years writing a biography of Martin Luther King and instead spend 24 years crafting a history of the civil rights movement in America with King as the centerpiece. A powerful trilogy about a tumultuous time of progress, reaction, and change

Caro, Robert. <u>The Years of Lyndon Johnson</u>.
The Path to Power. 1982. Knopf. 978-0394499734. 882pp.
Means of Ascent. 1990. Knopf. 978-0394528359. 560pp.
Master of the Senate. 2002. Knopf. 978-0394528366. 1,200pp.
The Passage of Power. 2012. Knopf. 978-0679405078. 736pp.

"Knowing Lyndon Baines Johnson . . . is essential to understanding the history of the United States in the twentieth century." In four extremely detailed and meticulously researched books, Caro examines the character of the man, the nature of personal and political power, and the evolving idea of America. Caro's lucid, vivid writing, and his apt selection of elements make enthralling and compelling reading. Caro has promised one more volume to conclude the story.

Manchester, William. <u>The Last Lion</u>.
The Last Lion: Winston Spencer Churchill: Visions of Glory, 1874–1932. 1983. Little, Brown and Company. 978-0316545037. 992pp.
The Last Lion: Winston Spencer Churchill: Alone, 1932–1940. 1988. Little, Brown and Company. 978-0316545129. 784pp.
The Last Lion: Winston Spencer Churchill: Defender of the Realm, 1940–1965. 2012. Little, Brown and Company. 978-0316547703. 1,232pp. Written with Paul Reid.

Filled with period details, historic sweep, and insights into power, Manchester's magnificent books about larger-than-life figure Winston Churchill are absorbing and considered by critics and readers to be "magisterial." The final book of the trilogy was completed (in fact almost entirely written) by author Paul Reid, Manchester's handpicked successor, and published eight years after Manchester's death.

McCullough, Colleen. <u>Masters of Rome</u>.
The First Man in Rome. 2008 (first published in 1990). William Morrow Paperbacks. 978-0061582417. 1,152pp. FICTION
The Grass Crown. 2008 (first published in 1991). William Morrow Paperbacks. 978-0061582394. 1,152pp. FICTION
Fortune's Favorites. 2008 (first published in 1993). William Morrow Paperbacks. 978-0061582400. 1,136pp. FICTION
Caesar's Women. 2008 (first published in 1996). William Morrow Paperbacks. 978-0061582424. 928pp. FICTION
Caesar: A Novel. 2003 (first published in 1997). Random House (paperback). 978-0099460435. 1,056pp. FICTION
The October Horse: A Novel of Caesar and Cleopatra. 2007 (first published in 2002). Simon & Schuster (paperback). 978-1416566656. 800pp. FICTION
Antony and Cleopatra: A Novel. 2008 (first published in 2007). Simon and Schuster (paperback). 978-1416552956. 576pp. FICTION

McCullough, best known for the 1977 Australian blockbuster *The Thorn Birds*, offers readers a lifetime reading plan with her evolving series of books about Rome near the end of the republic and the epic personalities who ruled, or tried to rule, there. Full of drama and detail, meticulously researched, these books are engrossing and demand a high commitment of time, attention, and upper-body strength.

Shaara, Michael and Jeff Shaara. <u>Civil War Trilogy</u>.

Gods and Generals. 1997. Ballantine Books (paperback). 978-0345409577. 512pp. FICTION

The Killer Angels: A Novel of the Civil War. 1996 (originally published in 1974). Ballantine Books (paperback). 978-0345407276. 368pp. FICTION

The Last Full Measure. 1999. Ballantine Books (paperback). 978-0345425 485. 576pp. FICTION

The Killer Angels, a novel about the Battle of Gettysburg, was published in 1974 and quickly won critical and popular acclaim as well as the Pulitzer Prize for fiction. After Michael Shaara's death, his son Jeff—also a writer of historical fiction—continued the Civil War story. *Gods and Generals* precedes the Battle of Gettysburg and *The Last Full Measure* relates the final two years of the war. This is historical fiction at its finest, historically accurate, and emotionally gripping.

Unusual Tellings—Books with Unique Narrative Structures

If straightforward, chronological history is not your style, explore these unusual tellings. Each of the books on this list, a mix of fiction and nonfiction, offers history told in a unique narrative style and voice.

Binet, Laurent.

HHhH. 2009. Farrar, Straus and Giroux. 978-0374169916. 327pp. FICTION.

"Once again I find myself frustrated by my genre's constraints," says the narrator of this remarkable historical novel. But Binet, the author, can make no such complaint. Telling the story of the 1942 assassination of Nazi Reinhard Heydrich "the Butcher of Prague," Binet moves effortlessly between the past and the present, between fiction and history, and between lyricism and documentation. The result is a novel that grabs you with its unusual narrative style, presents a story with rising tension, and offers a history lesson on a lesser-known episode of World War II. Translated from the French, this is Binet's first book.

Brown, Craig.

Hello Goodbye Hello: A Circle of 101 Remarkable Meetings. 2012. Simon & Schuster. 978-1451683608. 356pp.

British author Brown uses 1001 words to narrate each meeting between two famous figures. The gimmick is that each meeting connects with the previous and the next meeting—Salvador Dali met Freud, Freud met Mahler, Mahler met Rodin, Rodin met Isadora Duncan, who met Jean Cocteau who met Charlie Chaplin—the circle of 101 starts and ends with Adolph Hitler and surprisingly includes Michael Jackson, Leo Tolstoy, and Leonard Cohen among others. The meetings were often prosaic, but the participants are all noteworthy. Gossipy, sly, and thought-provoking, this is a most unusual way to think about biography and the unexpected interweaving of history.

Galeano, Eduardo.

▶ *Mirrors: Stories of Almost Everyone.* 2009. Nation Books (paperback). 978-1568586120. 391pp.

Uruguayan journalist and author Galeano blends history, journalism, lyricism, storytelling, and commentary in this poetic and playful book that offers a history of the world while paying great attention to the emotional, human, and psychic meaning of events. Short paragraphs take the reader through the human moments that we call history from the beginning of time to the end of the 20th century. Galeano effortlessly includes parts of the globe and groups of people often ignored by the standard Western view. Galeano is well known for the *Memory of Fire Trilogy*, an equally poetic history of Latin America.

Gombrich, E. H.

A Little History of the World. 2005. Yale. 978-0300108835. 304pp. Ⓨ Ⓐ

This charming survey covers the history of the entire world from prehistory to World War I in gentle prose and broad strokes that are nonetheless accurate and acute. Gombrich, an Austrian, wrote *A Little History of the World* in German in 1936 and it was not translated into English until 2001. Intended for children, all readers will be entertained and informed by this humane book.

Morris, Edmund.

Dutch: A Memoir of Ronald Reagan. 1999. Random House. 03946555082. 876pp.

Morris upset critics in 1999 with this official biography that incorporates an imaginary narrator and some flights of fancy to tell the life story of President Ronald Reagan. The book was a best seller on the nonfiction list, but is it a fictionalized biography or biographical fiction? Morris had great access to Reagan in the White House and after the presidency up to Reagan's diagnosis with Alzheimer's. He presents a well-defined portrait of the character of the man in an unorthodox and unexpected telling.

Wolff, Daniel.

How Lincoln Learned to Read: Twelve Great Americans and the Educations that Made Them. 2010. Bloomsbury (paperback). 978-1608190379. 345pp. Ⓨ Ⓐ

In this unusual approach to both biography and American history, author Wolff tells the life stories of such diverse Americans as Ben Franklin, Elvis

Presley, Sarah Winnemucca, and W.E.B. Du Bois. By looking at their early years, Wolff seeks to understand how each found "their way to knowledge," whether through formal schooling like Jack Kennedy or the harsh practicalities of slavery like Sojourner Truth. Each essay in Wolff's book can stand alone as a biographical essay about the intellectual life of a great American.

Zusak, Marcus. ♟
The Book Thief. 2006. Knopf. 978-0375831003. 560pp. FICTION ⓎⒶ
A dark book that is strangely uplifting, *The Book Thief* takes place in Nazi Germany where nine-year-old Liesl is growing up as a stealer of books. Her young life is disrupted but also created by the chaos around her—war, bombings, the Holocaust, and Death—who, it turns out, is the narrator of the novel. Zusak is an Australian author and his book is an international best seller translated into 30 languages and as intriguing to grown-ups as to young adults.

Just the Facts, Ma'am—Curling up with a Good Reference Book

Admit it. Sometimes, you like to curl up with a big fat reference book and just browse. It's a way of discovering ideas, reminding yourself of things you already know, and exploring issues you've never encountered before. Before the online availability of all the world's knowledge, reference books were the way to go. Here is an assortment of one-volume reference books that still deliver the goods. Don't keep these on the reference shelf, share them with readers!

Bell, Dana.
Smithsonian Atlas of World Aviation: Charting the History of Flight from the First Balloons to Today's Most Advanced Aircraft. 2008. Smithsonian. 978-006125144. 230pp.
From balloons to blimps to Boeing, this comprehensive look at the international history of aviation is abundantly illustrated and full of insider information like how runways are numbered and how flight charts are created. Bell looks at aviation in war and in peace and offers brief essays about famous aviation moments and personalities. The author was formerly with the Smithsonian's National Air and Space Museum and has written numerous other books about the history of flight.

Dent, Susie, editor.
Brewer's Dictionary of Phrase and Fable, 19th Edition. 2012. Hodder. 978-0550102454. 1,480pp.
More than a dictionary, less than an encyclopedia, *Brewer's* has been published since 1870 providing serious scholars and casual browsers with brief, erudite explanations of historical, cultural, and literary references. *Brewer's*

should be the companion of all history buffs. It offers readers the ultimate experience of serendipity as you discover things you didn't even know you wanted to know.

Grun, Bernard and Eva Simpson.
The Timetables of History: A Horizontal Linkage of People and Events. 2005. Touchstone. 978-0743270038. 848pp.

Did you know that spectacles were invented in 1290; Talleyrand and Louis XVI were born in the same year (1754), or that absolutely nothing of note occurred in 1418? This unique book addresses the simultaneity of history—who did what, when, and what else was going at the same time. Each moment of the past is multifaceted and this volume proves it. Laid out in a grid format with rows for years and columns for broad categories like politics, culture, arts, science, and "daily life." The focus is international, though there is an emphasis on Western Europe and the Americas. This volume is a tantalizing miscellany of factoids that will lead you to further exploration.

Hart-Davis, Adam.
▶ *History: The Definitive Visual Guide (from the Dawn of Civilization to the Present Day).* 2007. Dorling-Kindersley. 978-0756631192. 612pp.

Starting with the earliest ancestors of mankind, this oversized, family-friendly book provides international scope and interdisciplinary coverage to look at all of history. Lavishly illustrated, the treatment given to history is broad, not deep, but in their trademark visually stunning way, publisher Dorling Kindersley provides a compelling look at the story of humanity on the earth. This beautiful book is a starting place for any exploration of the past; definitely a coffee table book—it's too big for a lap.

King, Russell, editor.
Atlas of Human Migration. 2007. Firefly. 978-1554072873. 192pp.

The movement of humans around the world is a narrative that runs throughout history—the scale is global and the time frame is endless. For much of history, human migration was an uncounted phenomenon—national boundaries shifted, official documents didn't exist, and people just moved. Concise essays discuss the major movements of peoples throughout history starting with the first exodus of humanity out of Africa and progressing chronologically through the migrations of seekers looking for a better environment, kinder treatment, religious and intellectual freedom, or greater economic opportunity. Includes time lines, photographs, and maps.

Ovenden, Mark.
Railway Maps of the World. 2011. Viking. 978-0670022656. 138pp.

Transportation, cartography, and graphic design came together to provide the traveling public with a visual way to understand their options for train travel. Heavily illustrated with travel posters and historic maps of international railroads, the book has minimal text, a nice bibliography, a webography, and an international list of rail museums. This is the perfect armchair travel book for history readers and those nostalgic for the rails.

First Person Historical—The Fictional Lives of Real People

These entertaining novels offer a mash-up of history, biography, memoir, and fiction. Each protagonist was a real person and all of these novels offer strong first-person narration and vibrant historical settings.

Benjamin, Melanie.
▶ *The Autobiography of Mrs. Tom Thumb.* 2012. Bantam (paperback). 978-0385344166. 480pp. FICTION

A 19th-century woman with feminine beauty, Lavinia Warren Bump left a happy but provincial life of probable spinsterhood to become a performer. Her talent was that she was small. Born with proportional dwarfism, Vinnie was two feet, eight inches tall, but she possessed a large personality, innate dignity, and the optimistic spirit of her era—the Gilded Age. When she finally teamed up with P.T. Barnum, the world met her. Benjamin creates a terrific portrait of Vinnie and her equally small sister Minnie traveling with the circus, socializing with Astors and Roosevelts, and working with Barnum. Benjamin is also the author of *Alice Have I Been* (2009) about Alice Liddell who was the inspiration for *Alice in Wonderland* and *The Aviator's Wife* (2013) about Anne Morrow Lindbergh.

Dean, Michael.
I, Hogarth. 2013. Overlook. 978-1468303421. 272pp. FICTION

William Hogarth, visual chronicler of English society and mores, filled his paintings and engravings with recognizable places in London. He depicted the economic lives of laboring men and working women, showed the aristocracy at play, and satirized the political life of his day. Author Michael Dean transports the reader into the mindset and milieu of 18th-century England offering Hogarth as the bawdy and energetic narrator of his own tempestuous life as an artist; a protector of creative rights; a lusty rake; a devoted, if flawed, husband; and a sincere man.

Graves, Robert.
I, Claudius: From the Autobiography of Tiberius Claudius Born 10 B.C. Murdered and Deified A.D. 54. 1989 (originally published in 1934). Vintage (paperback). 978-0679724773. 468pp. FICTION

In the year 41, Rome gained its most unlikely emperor, the stammering, drooling Claudius—uncle of the recently dead and much reviled Caligula. This classic historical novel, first published in 1934, gives us Claudius, Emperor of Rome from AD 41 to 54, in his own words. Physically handicapped and considered a fool, he was ridiculed and dismissed by the more powerful members of his scheming family. He filled his time with books and learning, and staying out of the line of sight of ambitious and deadly relatives, like his "remarkable" but "abominable" grandmother, Livia. But Claudius observed, understood, and remembered all. Graves offers us Claudius's "confidential history" of the family whose business was the running of the Roman Empire.

Miles, Rosalind.
I, Elizabeth: A Novel. 2003 (originally published in 1994). Broadway (paperback). 978-0609809105. 656pp. FICTION ᵧ△

The years before Elizabeth became queen were fraught with tension as the young woman—a king in her heart, a bastard to the world—waited and watched to see who her enemies were, who supported her regal claim, and how royal events would play out—would she rule or die like her mother, beheaded as a traitor to the crown. Miles gives us events in Elizabeth's own imagined words of the years leading up to her rule and the personal dramas she endured during her reign as one of England's most glorious and long-reigning monarchs. Miles includes a helpful list of "The Persons of My History" that aids readers in keeping the players straight.

Sharp, Adrienne.
The True Memoirs of Little K. 2010. Farrar, Strauss and Giroux. 978-0374207304. 373pp. FICTION

A 99-year-old woman sits in an apartment in Paris and tells her story: "I was the lover of two grand dukes, the mistress of the tsar. The last tsar." As a 17-year-old rising star, ballerina Mathilde Kschessinska set her sights on the young *tsarevitch*, Nicholas. What followed was a life of glamour and tumult at the edges of both the Romanov court and the Russian Revolution. The imperial world of St. Petersburg and the artistic world of the ballet are detailed through the distinct voice of a passionate woman who went after what she wanted and then survived the destruction of it all.

Chapter Five

Mood/Tone

We often read fiction to feel something—humor, joy, sadness, clarity. Nonfiction has the same power to create a feeling or mood in the reader. Historians can immerse readers in a mood from history like the anxiety of a time when money became meaningless as in Adam Fergusson's *When Money Dies* or the exuberance of a global theme like travel and exploration in Joyce Chaplin's *Round About the Earth*. Historians can also take a certain point of view and craft their research and prose to offer us humor or tragedy, to show man at his best or worse, and even to speculate about what might have happened in the past and how that would have altered our present. The following books offer readers the feelings from history.

Conflict—One-volume Wars

Perhaps, it is an impossible mission to tell the story of a war in one volume, yet authors continue to attempt it and many achieve critical and popular success with their efforts. These volumes offer a starting point for understanding some of history's major conflicts.

Ferling, John E.
▶ *Almost a Miracle: The American Victory in the War of Independence.* 2007. Oxford. 978-0195181210. 704pp.
It was George Washington himself who suggested it was almost a miracle the revolutionaries won their fight against the better-armed and better-trained soldiers of England. In this immense narrative, Ferling shows how victory,

never guaranteed, came about. Taking a chronological approach, he offers a very readable survey of the military history, the personalities, and the social world of America in the dramatic and formative war years from 1775 to 1783.

Gaddis, John Lewis.
The Cold War: A New History. 2005. Penguin. 978-1594200625. 352pp.
When World War II ended in 1945, a new era could have started, but the coalition of Allies that had worked together for victory—England, Russian, and the United States—remained at war, ". . . ideologically and geopolitically, if not militarily." When the World War ended, the Cold War began. Historian and professor Gaddis had a goal to write a brief version of the events, players, and meanings of the Cold War so his students, many born after the Berlin Wall fell, could understand the conflict. This concise volume offers an overview of the war that never got "hot" but that lasted for almost 50 years.

Halberstam, David.
The Coldest Winter: America and the Korean War. 2007. Hyperion. 140130 0529. 719pp.
David Halberstam was an award-winning journalist who wrote equally compelling books about war and about sports. This, his final work, is an authoritative look at America's forgotten war—the Korean War. Halberstam had the opportunity to interview many participants of the conflict and has interwoven their battle stories and memories with the larger narrative of the international politics that created the war. Halberstam's classic about the Vietnam War *The Best and the Brightest* published in 1972 is still highly recommended.

Hanson, Victor Davis.
A War Like No Other: How the Athenians and Spartans Fought the Peloponnesian War. 2005. Random House. 978-1400060955. 416pp.
"The Peloponnesian War is now 2,436 years in the past. Yet Athens and Sparta are still on our minds and will not go away." Hanson offers a thematic approach (Fear, Fire, Disease, Terror, Armor, Horses, Ships, etc.) to this fifth-century civil war that engulfed Greece, and was comparable to modern wars in Vietnam, the Balkans, or the Middle East—brutal, prolonged, and often chaotic; involving citizens; shifting alliances, terror, and attrition; as well as all out land and sea battles. A brilliant exploration of a seminal event in the past, Hanson puts a lifetime of study and thought into this volume.

Hastings, Max.
Inferno: The World at War 1939–1945. 2011. Knopf. 978-0307273598. 729pp.
Hastings, an accomplished military historian, has written the story of world war from the bottom up, from the perspectives of the "little people rather than the big ones." The result is an excellent one-volume history of World War II that tells how the people, not just the soldiers and generals, suffered or

survived. This is military history combined with people's history and written by a master. Hastings was the recipient of the 2012 Pritzker Military Library Literature Award for Lifetime Achievement in Military Writing.

McPherson, James M. ♟

Battle Cry of Freedom: The Civil War Era (Oxford History of the United States). 1988. Oxford. 978-0195038637. 904pp.

Renowned historian McPherson explicates the causes of the Civil War and details many of the battles and their aftermath. Impeccable scholarship, a flowing narrative, and great humanity make this an important book and a compelling read. Acknowledged by most critics as perhaps the best one-volume treatment of the Civil War, this title is Volume 6 of the Oxford History of the United States series—11 books by major scholars encompassing the entire political, social, and cultural history of America.

Meyer, G. J.

A World Undone: The Story of the Great War, 1914 to 1918. 2006. Delacorte. 978-0553803549. 704pp.

Known at the time as The Great War, the world had never experienced such an all-encompassing and deadly conflict. Meyer provides an absorbing overview with chapters about the key moments, people, and progress of the war along with illuminating background essays on this war's international themes, historical reasons, and peccadilloes (like the futility of the trenches, the introduction of technology to warfare, or the "dysfunctional brotherhood" of the British commanders). This is excellent popular history with depth and substance providing a forceful depiction of the scope and destruction of the "war to end all wars."

Wedgwood, C. V.

The Thirty Years War. 2005 (originally published in 1938). NYRB (paperback). 978-1590171462. 536pp.

The Foreword to this volume refers to Wedgewood as the "greatest narrative historian of her century" and a writer who "told complex stories in precise, human terms." In this brilliant work of narrative history written in England in the 1930s, Wedgewood provides a story line for the conflicts that encompassed Europe from 1618 to 1648, a war created by monarchs, fought by mercenaries, and endured by peasants, clergy, and all the people—a war that "need not have happened" that "settled nothing worth settling." This is a history classic.

It Was the Worst of Times—History as Horror Story

Man's inhumanity to man is a recurring theme in history. These sad but compelling books show the big picture of some of humanities darker moments.

Applebaum, Anne. 🏆
▶ *Gulag: A History.* 2003. Doubleday. 0767900561. 677pp.

From the Russian Revolution in 1918 through Stalin's expansion in the 1950s until their dissolution under Gorbachev in 1986, millions of Soviet citizens were arbitrarily arrested, dehumanized, and imprisoned in inconceivably harsh conditions in remote forced-labor camps. The camps, at least one in every time zone in Russia, created a parallel Soviet society isolating dissident opinions and supplying slave labor to advance the Soviet Union's mid-century industrialization efforts. Applebaum makes effective use of camp memoirs and newly available archival material in this spellbinding and compassionate book about a horrifying example of man's institutionalized inhumanity to his fellow man and a government's attack on its own people.

Chang, Iris.
The Rape of Nanking: The Forgotten Holocaust of World War II. 1997. Basic Books. 0465068359. 290pp.

This best-selling book was both lauded and criticized, but all agreed that it reawakened awareness of a forgotten episode of war. In December 1937, Nanking, the capital city of Chiang Kai-shek's Nationalist China, fell to the Japanese. The Japanese didn't just occupy the city, they terrorized and brutalized the people—mass executions of men, gang rape and forced prostitution of women, and citizens beaten, beheaded, bayoneted, and burned. This historical episode of cruelty and ferocity—a World War II atrocity that Chang equates with the Holocaust and the bombing of Hiroshima—is very forcefully detailed in this book, not recommended for gentle readers.

Demos, John.
The Enemy Within: 2000 Years of Witch-hunting in the Western World. 2008. Viking. 978-0670019991. 336pp.

"Always and everywhere, charges of witchcraft were grounded in a web of local, intensely personal relations." Witch hunts aren't generally about witchcraft. Demos, a professor and expert on the Salem witch trials, looks at the "ubiquity, the near universality of witch-hunting" in human history. His journey begins in Rome as Christianity grows and spreads, travels through the drama of European witch-hunting, and ends in late 20th-century Massachusetts where he finds parallels between day-care abuse accusations and historic witch hunts. This is an overview not of a time but of a phenomenon. Though his prose and his arguments retain an academic tenor, Demos is writing for general readers; his tone is compassionate and his content thought-provoking. For another look at socially sanctioned persecution, read *God's Jury: The Inquisition and the Making of the Modern World* (2012) by Cullen Murphy.

Gourevitch, Philip et al.
We Wish to Inform You That Tomorrow We Will be Killed with Our Families: Stories from Rwanda. 1998. Farrar, Straus and Giroux. 0374286973. 353pp.

In 1994, the ruling Hutu majority in Rwanda murdered more than 800,000 of their countrymen. Working from lists of names, using machetes to hack people to death, the murders of the Tutsis people in Rwanda were methodical and encouraged by the government. Because this story is such recent history, Gourevitch—a writer with the New Yorker—writes in a style that is reportage. He uses interviews with survivors and traveled to the sites of many of the killings. He tells a story that ranks alongside the 20th century's other horrific genocides like the Holocaust, the murder of the Armenians, Pol Pot's destruction in Cambodia, the partition of India, and others.

Kelly, John.
The Graves Are Walking: The Great Famine and the Saga of the Irish People.
2012. Henry Holt and Company. 978-0805091847. 397pp.

One million dead, two million fled, one in three people just no longer there—Ireland from 1845 to 1847 became a ghost country. Dependence on one crop, the potato, made the food supply vulnerable and when the potato crop failed, people died. The British government supplied relief, but political ideology overrode humanity and the goal became social change and not compassionate lifesaving. Some of history's most heartbreaking stories are about poverty and starvation in Ireland during the Great Famine. Kelly shines a bright light on it all in this compassionate reexamination.

Rediker, Marcus.
The Slave Ship: A Human History. 2007. Viking. 978-0670018239. 432pp.

From the late 1500s to the late 1800s, 12.4 million souls were pulled from their native African land and sent on a journey that would culminate in lifetime servitude if they survived the trip, and many did not. Employed to carry out this "filthy business" were hardened ship's crews and their tough ship captains—men who generally displayed the most brutish and deplorable aspects of mankind. *The Slave Ship* focuses on the journey where human beings were a commodity and fortunes could be made by a captain with the resolve to degrade and subjugate other men and women. A beautifully written book about a most distressing event in the human past—a must-read.

Schama, Simon.
Citizens: A Chronicle of the French Revolution. 1990. Vintage (paperback).
978-0679726104. 976pp.

For 10 years, France—home of the Enlightenment and rational thinking—became a setting of social, cultural, political, and intellectual upheaval as the revolution erupted and then devolved into a reign of terror. The original goals of citizens' rights and *liberté, egalité, fraternité* gave way to massacre, as revolutionaries were now deemed enemies of the new state and anyone thought to be a counterrevolutionary was put to a bloody death by guillotine. Although this book is now more than 20 years old, Schama's vivid writing still enthralls as he presents the panorama of the French Revolution through personalities, anecdotes, and details.

If Only—Alternative Histories

> The road not taken belongs on the map.
> —Robert Cowley

The what-if and if-only moments of history are intriguing and slightly mind bending. What if Hitler had won? What if the Union had lost? What if we could travel back in time and change events? Historians and fiction authors love to play with the "What if" of the past.

Chabon, Michael. ♛
The Yiddish Policemen's Union. 2007. Harper. 978-0007149827. 432pp. FICTION

The displaced Jews of World War II—the "Frozen Chosen"—are resettled in Alaska instead of Israel, their 60-year grace period is almost up, and a seemingly motiveless murder has down-on-his-luck cop Meyer Landsman and his half-Tlingit, half-Jewish partner investigating. A hard-boiled Yiddish noir, a truly unique story taking a "what-if" premise from a real suggestion by FDR that Alaska be offered to the Jews as a homeland. Chabon is a smart, playful writer. If you like his approach, follow up with *The Amazing Adventures of Kavalier and Clay* (2000).

Cowley, Robert, editor.
The Collected What If? Eminent Historians Imagine What Might Have Been. 2006. Putnam. 978-0399152382. 827pp.

"What ifs can lead us to question long-held assumptions . . . define true turning points . . . show that small accidents or split-second decisions are as likely to have major repercussions as large ones." Robert Cowley offers readers the mind-expanding intellectual exercise of counterfactual history as undertaken by serious and respected historians like James Bradley, Stephen E. Ambrose, Cecelia Holland, David McCullough, and Alistair Horne. This edition unites into one book the essays from Volume 1 that concentrated on military history and Volume 2 that combined military and nonmilitary events.

Greenfield, Jeff.
Then Everything Changed: Stunning Alternate Histories of American Politics: JFK, RFK, Carter, Ford, Reagan. 2011. Putnam. 978-0399157066. 448pp.

"What would have happened if small twists of fate had given us different leaders, with different beliefs, strengths and weaknesses?" Greenfield, an accomplished journalist and political analyst, asks this question, then offers three retellings of recent political history to show how things could have been different. Greenfield argues that his scenarios have "plausibility" and his alternative takes on John Kennedy, Robert Kennedy, and Gerald Ford offer much to think about.

King, Stephen. ♛
11/23/62. 2011. Scribner. 978-1451627282. 849pp. FICTION

If you could time travel to Dallas 1962 and prevent the assassination of President Kennedy, would you? More importantly, could you? The past might fight you in its efforts to stay the way it was. Modern day Maine high-school teacher Jake Epping learns he can go back in time to 1958 and live in the past until the moment is right to try to stop Lee Harvey Oswald, save Kennedy, and change history. King's acute portrayal of the 1950s and 1960s make this seem like historical fiction, but the time travel premise makes it a "what-if" book.

Mason, Phil.
Napoleon's Hemorrhoids: And Other Small Events that Changed History. 2009. Skyhorse. 978-1602397644. 253pp.

Mason offers true moments from the past that, had things been slightly different, might have resulted in history playing out another way. Anecdotal and lightly presented, some of the moments may be known, but others are a surprise—like Napoleon's hemorrhoids affecting his performance at Waterloo and Queen Victoria nearly being shot by a boy hunting birds when she was a baby. An entertaining look at what could have been.

Roth, Philip. ♛
▶ *The Plot against America.* 2004. Houghton Mifflin. 0618509283. 400pp. FICTION ⬒

When Charles Lindbergh wins the 1940 presidential election and keeps America out of World War II, Fascism in the United States rises and a Jewish family in New Jersey fights to survive. A novel that reads like a first-person memoir, Roth is so conversational and intimate that you have to remind yourself he is writing fiction about a possible American past and not narrating what really happened.

Turtledove, Harry.
Hitler's War: The War That Came Early, v. 1. 2009. Del Rey. 978-0345491824. 496pp. FICTION

Germany invades Czechoslovakia in 1938 instead of Poland in 1939 and world history is rewritten. Turtledove is an acknowledged master of alternate history and an author with a large fan base. This is a fast-paced and exciting novel with a large cast of characters relating events from multiple viewpoints. This alternate version of World War II continues in *West and East* (2010), *The Big Switch* (2011), and *Coup d'etat* (2012).

Willis, Connie. ♛
The Doomsday Book. 1993. Spectra. 978-0553562736. 592pp. FICTION [Y][A]

In 2048, an Oxford history student time travels to 1348 right into the maelstrom of the Black Death. Meanwhile, in her own time, a flu epidemic is wreaking havoc and endangering her return to the modern world. Willis has many fans of her witty, atmospheric, time-bending novels that put modern thinkers into historical moments. *Blackout* (2010) and *All Clear* (2010) are her more recent works about future historians time-traveling back into the turmoil of the London Blitz.

Be Afraid, Be Very Afraid—History as Cautionary Tale

Do you like horror stories? Some authors can look at the past and see danger for the future. Don't read these books alone at night.

Fergusson, Adam.
When Money Dies: The Nightmare of Deficit Spending, Devaluation, and Hyperinflation in Weimar Germany. 2010 (first published in 1975). Public Affairs. 978-1586489946. 269pp.

What happens if a government prints so much money that it no longer has any value? In 1975, Fergusson looked backward to Weimar Germany in the years between the World Wars to examine what happens: "theft was preferable to starvation; warmth was finer than honour, clothing more essential than democracy, food more needed than freedom." Fergusson asserts he isn't making predictions but argues this lesson from history could be read as a moral tale that proves "if you wish to destroy a nation you must first corrupt its currency."

Fraser, Evan D. G. and Andrew Rimas.
Empires of Food: Feast, Famine and the Rise and Fall of Civilizations. 2010. Free Press. 978-1439101896. 302pp.

Will earth's thin layer of soil continue to sustain the growth of our food? Will climate change alter what we eat? Growing, storing, and trading food have been critical to the expansion of human population on earth, but relying on limited crops and trusting that the environment will always support growth may not continue to work. Like all empires, the empire of food will undoubtedly decline and fall—can we prepare for that day? Canadian scholars Fraser and Rimas explore the possibilities. Along the same lines as Michael Pollan's *Omnivore's Dilemma* (2006) and *Pandora's Seed* (2010) by Spencer Wells.

Linden, Eugene.
The Winds of Change: Climate, Weather, and the Destruction of Civilizations. 2006. Simon & Schuster. 978-0684863528. 302pp.

Earth's climate has always cycled and changed. When stable, it has resulted in advancement of civilization, global exploration, and excellent harvests leading to peace; but weather can also be unpredictable and destructive leading to famine, outbreaks of disease, and mass migrations. The weather will always be a factor in the human story. Environmental journalist Linden writes a thoughtful and scientifically based analysis of the impact of climate on the past and its potential impact on the future. For more about the impact of climate on history, explore the works of author Brian Fagan.

Markel, Howard.

When Germs Travel: Six Major Epidemics That Have Invaded America since 1900 and the Fears They Have Unleashed. 2004. Pantheon. 978-0375420955. 288pp.

Markel, a pediatrician and medical historian, documents the historical and contemporary stories of diseases that could potentially go rogue and kill us all—cholera, plague, tuberculosis, AIDS, trachoma, and typhus fever. Markel effectively mixes the personal and the historical in this book that offers a passionate call to action on global public health.

Morris, Ian. 🏆

▶ ***Why the West Rules—For Now: The Patterns of History, and What They Reveal About the Future.*** 2010. Farrar, Straus and Giroux. 978-0374290023. 768pp.

Why has "the West" (defined by Morris in broad terms) dominated world events? Morris argues that geography—not culture, technology, or personalities—allowed dominance, but it may not always remain so. This is a lucid and absorbing synthesis of a vast quantity of ideas and information made absorbing by Morris's humane approach, down-to-earth prose, deep scholarship, and inclusion and appreciation of popular culture. A delightfully thought-provoking book. Morris argues that the "important history" is global and evolutionary. Jared Diamond looks at similar ideas in his works *Guns, Germs and Steel* (1997) and *Collapse: How Societies Choose to Fail or Succeed* (2004)

Couth and Culture—Gentle Stories with No Battles or Blood

Tired of reading about war, kings, treachery, and the darker sides of the human story. Turn to these volumes for a look at the cultural side of humanity. Guaranteed to have no battles and no blood.

Ashenburg, Katherine.

▶ ***The Dirt on Clean: An Unsanitized History.*** 2007. North Point Press. 978-0865476905. 356pp.

The Dirt on Clean traces what it has meant to be clean through 2,000 years of human history. Different times and places have defined "clean" differently. Ancient Romans were content to cover themselves with oil and then scrape it from their bodies before bathing, while folks in the 17th century considered themselves clean if they just changed their linen undershirt. From public baths to the rise of the marketing of hygiene, Ashenburg's book is delightful, easygoing, informative, and fun.

Friedwald, Will.
Stardust Melodies: The Biography of Twelve of America's Most Popular Songs. 2002. Pantheon. 978-0375420894. 416pp.

Friedwald looks at 12 popular songs from 1914's *St Louis Blues* to *Lush Life*, written in 1938, and discusses how they came to be written, how they have been performed, and what they mean. Friedwald examines the musical structure of each song as well as the lyrics, the milieu of its creation, and its reception. The result is an unusual and engaging view of American popular culture in the first 40 years of the 20th century. For a look at 20th-century classical music, read Alex Ross's *The Rest is Noise: Listening to the Twentieth Century* (2008).

Grier, Katherine C.
Pets in America: A History. 2006. University of North Carolina Press. 0807829900. 392pp.

Is there anything more common than a songbird in a cage, a pampered house cat, or the family dog? It wasn't always so. The story of how animals that once had functions—hunting, mousing, herding, guarding, etc.—became house pets, members of the family, and objects of love, devotion, and delight is told in Grier's comprehensive social history. From the creation of a consumer pet industry in the form of pet stores, pet food companies, and pet accessories to cruelty prevention campaigns, the rise of small animal veterinary medicine, and the ongoing controversies of breeding, spaying, and neutering, Grier covers everything you want to know about the progress of all pets (not just cats and dogs) in America. Filled with illustrations of pampered pets. For another aspect of the relationship between Americans and their animals, read Virginia Dejohn Anderson's *Creatures of Empire: How Domestic Animals Transformed Early America* (2004).

Harris, Mark.
Pictures at a Revolution: Five Movies and the Birth of the New Hollywood. 2008. Penguin. 1594201528. 496pp.

In 1968, the five movies nominated for the Academy Award for Best Picture were *Bonnie and Clyde*, *The Graduate*, *In the Heat of the Night*, *Guess Who's Coming to Dinner*, and *Dr. Doolittle*. Two of these movies exemplified the old way of filmmaking, offering vehicles to aging stars and a staid style of storytelling. Three of these films offered a new business model for producing and bold explorations of original content and innovative cinematic style. Hollywood is huge in the ongoing story of American popular culture, and Harris, a former journalist with a deep understanding of film, tells the intriguing story of how in 1968, Hollywood reinvented itself yet again and became relevant to a new generation of creators and, most importantly, consumers.

Homans, Jennifer.
Apollo's Angels: A History of Ballet. 2010. Random House. 978-1400060603. 672pp.

The ethereal beauty of the ballet—a world of chiffon, sylphs, and graceful motion—is really a world of arduous dedication, unnatural movement, and single-minded drive. Homans, a former ballerina, knows her subject firsthand. From Renaissance beginnings to the French court where the king himself participated in the dances, to czarist Russia and Balanchine's America, Homan's follows the creative development of the dance. She is a beautiful prose stylist and an opinionated scrutinizer of the lively history and, in her analysis, limited future of ballet.

Marks, Craig and Rob Tannenbaum.
I Want my MTV: The Uncensored Story of the Music Video Revolution. 2011. Dutton. 978-0525952305. 608pp. Ⓨ Ⓐ

MTV was like a "national radio station with pictures." It gave music and emotion to young people, it became an international phenomenon almost from the moment of its launch in 1981, it burned white hot then died out by 1992—once the network shifted from its music video base. Started and staffed by inexperienced, but hopeful artists and executives, MTV's world of "quick cuts, celebrations of youth, shock value, impermanence, beauty—influenced not only music, but network and cable TV, radio, advertising, film, art, fashion, race, teen sexuality, even politics." This oral history does a great job showing the rapid arc of creation, unimagined success, and decline of MTV.

McCullough, David.
The Greater Journey: Americans in Paris. 2011. Simon & Schuster. 978-14165 71766. 576pp.

This is the biography of an experience—Americans living abroad. In the early 1800s, the first batch of true Americans—those born and raised after the Revolutionary War—began to see the world. Many went to Paris—a city of culture, education, and refinement. Among the travelers were artists, authors, and students. As American visitors were learning Paris's lessons about art, medicine, and good living, the city itself was being transformed by Haussmann and his construction crews and by the social and political change of the Paris Commune and the Second Empire. Early visitors paid homage to the still-living Marquise de Lafayette and by the end of the century, witnessed the Statue of Liberty being built. This unique story covering 1830–1900 includes minibiographies of many lives and is told with McCullough's trademark genial intelligence.

Nachman, Gerald.
Raised on Radio. 2000. University of California Press. 978-0520223035. 544pp.

Television didn't replace radio, but the abundance and breadth of radio programming was never the same after television's ascendency. In this relaxed and nostalgic traipse through the popular entertainment that captured a nation's imagination, Nachman celebrates the programs, performers, and common culture offered by radio. Nachman, a student of popular culture, has also written about Ed Sullivan and the rebel stand-up comedians of the 1950s and 1960s.

Walker, Brian.
The Comics: The Complete Collection. 2011. Abrams. 978-0810995956. 672pp.
Y A

Lie on the floor, stomach down, feet in the air, propped up on your elbows, and relive the Sunday morning experience of millions of American children—read your way through the funnies. This massive volume of beautifully reproduced comic strips lets you time travel through the images and humor of this 20th-century American art form. This oversized volume combines Walker's two previous works, *The Comics before 1945* and *The Comics since 1945*.

Old Stories for Young Readers—History Written for Children

Reliable and scholarly, but appropriate to their audience, these books written especially for young people have swift-moving prose, intriguing illustrations, and all the bibliographic apparatus you would expect in more academic works. They are excellent starting places for any topic and excellent options for readers who want a gentler description of the past.

Freedman, Russell.
Who Was First? Discovering the Americas. 2007. Clarion. 978-0618663910. 88p.

It turns out Christopher Columbus was a latecomer to the American shores. Freedman guides readers through the stories of America's other early discoverers like the Chinese and the Vikings. Russell Freedman is the unofficial dean of historical nonfiction for young readers. He is a well-respected researcher who crafts his material into serious, accessible books for young people. He has tackled many topics—Abraham Lincoln, Marion Anderson, World War I, Eleanor Roosevelt, the Declaration of Independence, and more.

Harness, Cheryl.
The Tragic Tale of Narcissa Whitman and a Faithful History of the Oregon Trail. 2006. National Geographic. 978-0792259206. 144p.

The sad story of missionary pioneers Marcus and Narcissa Whitman is told in a straightforward way, but what sets this book apart are Harness's pen-and-ink illustrations, a time line across the bottom of every page, sidebars, and a narrative style that is reader-friendly and very accessible. Harness has used the same approach writing about Myles Standish, Theodore Roosevelt, and Daniel Boone.

Heiligman, Deborah.
Charles and Emma: The Darwin's Leap of Faith. 2009. Henry Holt. 978-0805087215. 272pp.

 Charles Darwin struggled long and hard with his revolutionary ideas about science and evolution; he also struggled with the decision whether or not to marry. His future wife, Emma Wedgewood, also had doubts. She was a Christian who sincerely worried that because of his scientific beliefs, Darwin would go to hell and they would spend eternity apart. Despite their doubts, they took a chance on marriage and were devoted to each other and their children for a long life together. This book offers a lovely investigation of an adult relationship between two strong people with different beliefs and an exploration of how Darwin's personal life contributed to his scientific work.

Murphy, Jim.
Blizzard! The Storm That Changed America. 2006. Scholastic. 978-0590673105. 144p.

 On Saturday, March 12, 1888, the weather was unusually warm, few could predict that the worst snowstorm in recorded history was about to descend upon the eastern United States, crippling communication, transportation, and commerce and threatening every living thing from Canada down the coast to Virginia. All the pathos and triumphs are included in Murphy's book about one of the most dramatic weather events in recorded U.S. history.

Noon, Steve, illustrator and Philip Steele, author.
A City through Time: The Story of a City—From Ancient Colony to Vast Metropolis. 2013. DK. 978-1465402493. 49pp.

 This picture book traces the evolution of a Mediterranean city from its times as a Stone Age encampment through Greek colony, Roman, medieval, and Baroque city to industrial port and bustling modern metropolis. The illustrations are absorbing and have distinct details that illuminate the activities of each era. The sparse text connects the different times and shows the universal pattern of urban growth. Similar books include *A Port through Time* (2006), and *A Street through Time* (2013).

Pinkney, Andrea and Brian Pinkney.
Sit-in: How Four Friends Stood up by Sitting down. 2010. Little Brown. 0316070165. 40pp.

 In a picture book format, Pinkney tells the story of the 1960 Woolworth's lunch counter sit-in in Greensboro, North Carolina, where four young black college students sat down at the "whites only" counter and waited to be served. This is a gentle introduction for young readers to the civil rights struggle in America.

Sheinkin, Steve.
▶ *Which Way to the Wild West: Everything Your Schoolbooks Didn't Tell You about America's Westward Expansion.* 2009. Roaring Brook Press. 978-1596433212. 260pp.

Lighthearted, even irreverent, this anecdotal survey of the American Westward expansion hits the high points, but also includes less well-known characters and stories. A good list of sources will lead readers to more material. Sheinkin offers an excellent survey of a major movement in American history written to entertain and enlighten.

A How-to Guide—The Science, Art, and Craft of History

If you are interested in how historians "do" history, these books will tell you their secrets.

Burrow, John.
A History of Histories: Epics, Chronicles, Romances and Inquiries from Herodotus and Thucydides to the Twentieth Century. 2008. Knopf. 978-0375413117. 517p.

Is it the past that interests us or the crafted narratives we call "histories" that have captured our attention? Is the writing of history a science or an art? Scholar John Burrow has created a thoughtful and broad-minded look at the 2,500-year-old story of the writing of history in the West. This elegant and erudite book studies the writers who crafted the past into history and considers the works they presented to the world and that we still read today.

Childs, Craig.
Finders Keepers: A Tale of Archaeological Plunder and Obsession. 2010. Little Brown. 978-0316066426. 274pp.

Museum curators, scholars, treasure hunters, looters, private collectors, descendents, and people who make careers of digging up history are all interested in the potsherds and bones that comprise our record of the ancient past. Childs offers an archaeologist's point of view about museums, collections, and the joy, challenges, and ethics of finding and preserving the little broken pieces that tell so much and leave so much unexplained.

MacGregor, Neil.
▶ *A History of the World in 100 Objects: From the Handaxe to the Credit Card.* 2011. Viking. 978-0670022700. 707pp.

Can we engage with history by looking at things from the past? That is what museums ask us to do. MacGregor, curator of the British Museum, chose 100 objects from the museum's vast collections to illuminate themes in human history. Power, money, sex, and agriculture are explored by examining among other objects, a silver coin with the head of Alexander from 300 BC Turkey, a West African drum from the 1700s, and an early Victorian tea set. Based on the podcast series of the same name, this is an entertaining way to connect with history and think about how we think about the past.

MacMillan, Margaret.
Dangerous Games: The Uses and Abuses of History. 2010. Modern Library. 978-0812979961. 208pp.

We abuse, misuse, and ignore history at our own peril, according to MacMillan. This is an elegant, thought-provoking essay on the reasons why deliberate and well-crafted histories—works that accurately explain and describe the past—matter.

Pyne, Stephen J.
Voice and Vision: A Guide to Writing History and Other Serious Nonfiction. 2009. Harvard. 978-0674033306. 336pp.

A how-to book for those interested in writing history and narrative nonfiction. Pyne argues that history is both art and craft and shares tips for creating works that will entertain while they elucidate. Some of his advice includes don't leave things out and don't make things up.

Rabb, Theodore K.
The Last Days of the Renaissance: The March to Modernity. 2006. Basic Books. 0465068014. 246pp.

When did antiquity end? When did the world stop being medieval? When did things become modern? Humans continually try to understand the past in discrete chunks of definable time with true beginnings and endings. But the past wasn't really lived that way. Rabb, a professor at Princeton, looks at the shifts in society and thought that took place when the world shifted from medieval to renaissance and then when the way of thinking prevalent in the Renaissance gave way to modern thought. He offers a mind-expanding extended essay on how we look at the past.

Tuchman, Barbara.
Practicing History: Selected Essays. 1982. Ballantine. 978-0345303639. 320pp.

Tuchman was a private scholar who wrote beautifully and brilliantly on such diverse topics as World War I, the 14th century, and the American Revolution. Her essays speak directly to those interested in writing or reading history, reminding us that it is the fundamentals that matter: impeccable research, respect for the reader, entertaining writing, and clear unbiased thinking. This is an older book, but a classic of clear, precise writing and thinking.

Weir, William.
History's Greatest Lies: The Startling Truths Behind World Events Our History Books Got Wrong. 2009. Fair Winds Press (paperback). 1592333362. 288pp.

Did Nero really fiddle while Rome burned? Was Paul Revere the lone hero of that April night in 1775? Weir addresses well-known historical stories that persist even though they might not be true. Illustrated and easy to read, this book makes you rightfully question how history is done. Along the same vein, James W. Loewen takes on the lies and misreadings offered in history textbooks in *Lies My Teacher Told Me: Everything Your American History Textbook Got Wrong* (1996, revised 2007).

A Funny Thing Happened on the Way to the History Book—History with Humor

If you like your history with a light touch, try these books that see the humor in the past.

Holt, Jim.
Stop Me If You've Heard This: A History and Philosophy of Jokes. 2008. Norton. 978-0393066739. 141pp.

Jokes are more complicated than you realize. An area of folklore, along with myths, proverbs, nursery rhymes, and riddles, jokes are worthy of study for the insight they offer into the human psyche. Jokes subvert logic and play with language; they can be nice, naughty, inadvert, or deliberate; they provide a needed release of tension; but are often really little blasts of aggression toward women, minorities, or authority. Do new jokes get invented or have modern jokes just evolved from previous eras? Can we find a "general theory" of jokes? Should we bother? This brief, witty book is an extended essay that asks you to think about humor, history, and humanity.

Mallon, Thomas.
Watergate: A Novel. 2012. Pantheon. 978-0307378729. 448pp. FICTION

Politics becomes personal as Richard Nixon and his friends, enemies, and co-conspirators maneuver through the debacle of Watergate. What starts as "penny-ante crap" soon escalates to a political scandal that brings down a president. Mallon portrays it all as dark comedy with high stakes. Mallon is a bright and eclectic writer with a cool eye and a light touch. Also try *Henry and Clara* (1994), Mallon's historical novel about the young couple that accompanied the Lincolns to the theater.

Matyszak, Philip.
Legionary: The Roman Soldier's (Unofficial) Manual. 2009. Thames & Hudson. 978-0500251515. 224pp. ⓨⒶ

Would you like to run away and join the ancient Roman army? Before taking the leap, read this manual that will guide you through recruitment, equipage, training, campaigning, retirement, and burial. Backed by solid scholarship and written with lively wit, British scholar Matyszak—author of many other works about ancient Rome—tells all. If you find the legion isn't to your taste, try *Gladiator: The Roman Fighter's (Unofficial) Manual* (2011) also by Matyszak.

McBride, Tom and Ron Nief.
The Mindset Lists of American History: From Typewriters to Text Messages, What Ten Generations of Americans Think Is Normal. 2011. Wiley. 978-0470876237. 272pp. Y A

In 1998, two professors at Beloit College in Wisconsin published their first Mindset List. They hoped to help faculty connect with entering freshmen by reminding them that students born in 1980 hadn't witnessed the Challenger disaster and didn't understand the phrase "you sound like a broken record." Since then, Beloit has created lists covering other generations. This book looks at 150 years of American college student's cultural touchstones. Part nostalgia, part humor, and part sociology, the Mindset Lists remind us that each generation sees the world differently because their world is a different place.

Sass, Erik, Steve Wiegand, and the Editors of Mental Floss.
The Mental Floss History of the World: An Irreverent Romp through Civilization's Best Bits. 2008. Harper. 978-0060784775. 432pp.

Offering itself as a one-volume history of the world, this book is funny and substantial. While you won't find footnotes, an index, a bibliography, or anything else bespeaking academia or authority, you will discover "a wealth of fun facts . . . and maybe three-quarters of the 'important' stuff." This is a history survey course for hipsters and the rest of us—very readable and energetic. Brought to you by the editors of *Mental Floss* magazine ("where knowledge junkies get their fix").

Stewart, Jon, Ben Karlin, and David Javerbaum.
▶ *America (The Book): A Citizen's Guide to Democracy Inaction.* 2004. Warner Books. 0446532681. 227pp.

Satirist, political commentator, and television host Jon Stewart and his fellow wits from *The Daily Show* deliver a political primer written like a textbook with illustrations, sidebars, and timelines that educates as it skewers. Impudent and sassy, but basically grounded in fact, *America (The Book)* looks at the history and theory of democracy in America—how it came to be and how it could be better. Also enjoy Stewart's *Earth (The Book): A Visitor's Guide to the Human Race* (2010).

Vowell, Sarah.
The Wordy Shipmates. 2008. Riverhead. 978-1594489990. 254pp.

Writer and radio commentator Vowell likes to find out about things. Her explorations of American history are personal, conversational, and very droll. Here she turns her attention to the Puritans: "I'm always disappointed when I see the word 'Puritan' tossed around as shorthand for a bunch of generic, boring, stupid, judgmental killjoys. Because to me, they are very specific, fascinating, sometimes brilliant, judgmental killjoys." Vowel has also used her distinctive voice to write about the annexation of Hawaii in *Unfamiliar Fishes* (2011) and her odyssey visiting the sites of famous American deaths in *Assassination Vacation* (2005).

The Seven Ages of Man

Shakespeare knew what he was talking about when he described the seven ages of man: infancy, childhood, lover, soldier, middle age, dementia, and death. These books lean toward social science, philosophy, and social history and each offers an historical round up of a stage of life we all will pass through.

Abbott, Elizabeth.
A History of Mistresses. 2010. Overlook. 978-1590204436. 528pp.
    The Other Woman is a figure with a powerful, if hidden, place in history and literature. Abbot uses famous mistresses of the past and the present to explore the history and reality of marriage and relationships of men and women. Hagar from the Bible, royal lovers Nell Gwynn and Camilla Parker Bowles, artists like Maria Callas and Marilyn Monroe, and the secret lovers of politicians, gangsters, and others are all examined in this extensive and compulsively readable survey. Canadian professor Abbott has published several books that delve into the affairs of men and women, read *A History of Marriage* (2011) and *A History of Celibacy* (2000) to continue the exploration.

Bellesiles, Michael A.
A People's History of the U.S. Military: Ordinary Soldiers Reflect on Their Experience of War, from the American Revolution to Afghanistan. 2012. The New Press. 978-1595586285. 375pp.
    Using letters, memoirs, diaries, film, tale, and blogs, Bellesiles presents the experience of the common American soldier—what they experienced, how they felt, what they thought, etc. An intimate look into the mind and duties of a soldier.

Cassidy, Tina.
Birth: The Surprising History of How We Are Born. 2006. Atlantic Monthly. 978-0871139382. 312pp.
    Midwives, birthing stools, doulas, the Apgar score, the 19th-century controversy over hand washing, and the Lamaze method—the history of the human journey from inside a mother's body to the waiting arms of the world makes for fascinating, albeit sometimes grisly reading. Cassidy brings a journalist's sense of pacing and an eye for the telling anecdote to this social and medical history about the process of birth.

Cohen, Patricia.
In Our Prime: The Invention of Middle Age. 2012. Scribner. 978-1416572893. 306pp.
    People have always lived through the long expanse of adulthood that we now call middle age—the years of no longer young but not yet old. It is only recently and in America that those years became defined and layered with expectations. Cohen looks at how changing family patterns, advertisers, health

faddists, and people themselves created a new human developmental stage. Cohen describes her book as the "biography of the idea of middle age."

Mintz, Steven.
▶ *Huck's Raft: A History of American Childhood.* 2004. Harvard. 0674015088. 445pp.

Though the fictional Huck was an abused child, his raft represents an ideal of freedom, exploration, and self-discovery that remains the dream of childhood. Mintz, a cultural historian and professor, takes a survey approach as he looks at the realities of children's lives from Puritan days to the invention of teenagers in the 1930s to the modern dilemmas of hurried childhoods and overarching parental anxiety. This is a compassionate and compelling look at the history of American childhood.

Shenk, David.
The Forgetting: Alzheimer's: Portrait of an Epidemic. 2003. Anchor (paperback). 978-0385498388. 305pp.

The approaching epidemic of Alzheimer's disease is just beginning to impinge upon the aging world population. Shenk intersperses the history of this disease with discussions of some of the famous people who in retrospect were undoubtedly afflicted (Ralph Waldo Emerson, Jonathan Swift, Frederick Law Olmstead, Ronald Reagan, and Willem de Kooning) and he projects the bleak future where those who don't get the disease must still bear witness as it effects the economy, families, and society. Shenk's account of the slow journey to scientific knowledge and the upcoming storm is straightforward, sympathetic, and sobering.

Taylor, Timothy.
The Buried Soul: How Humans Invented Death. 2002. Beacon Press. 0807046728. 353pp.

What does it mean that humans bury bodies? Taylor, an archaeologist, looks at death and the rituals that surround it, specifically how bodies have been laid to rest, since prehistory. Taylor is equally enthralled by Viking burials, Aztec sacrifices, Lenin's corpse, bog bodies, and the prehistoric bones of babies found in a cave. Taylor mixes the historic, scientific, and personal in this fascinating, slightly gruesome work that is definitely not recommended for gentle readers.

Global Themes—Surveys of History's Big Topics

Some topics have affected us all—the propensity of humans to congregate in cities, the mysteries of the night, the instinct to trade and explore our planet, and the development of language, economic systems, and finance. These books offer large looks at the big topics that have shaped and challenged mankind.

Appleby, Joyce.
The Relentless Revolution: History of Capitalism. 2010. Norton. 978-0393068948. 494pp.

With unassailable scholarship but absolutely accessible narrative, Appleby romps through hundreds of years of economic history covering the entire globe. Arguing that capitalism is more social and cultural than economic or political and that its rise was never inevitable, Appleby lays out what capitalism is and how it has morphed over its life span.

Bernstein, William J.
A Splendid Exchange: How Trade Shaped the World. 2008. Atlantic Monthly. 978-0871139795. 477pp.

From the Silk Road to the Spice Islands to the Battle in Seattle, trade—buying, selling, bartering, and transporting commodities—has been one of mankind's primary endeavors. Politics, economics, cultural preferences, and personal taste, all have a place in this broad narrative history about a primal human impulse that has propelled international prosperity and fostered intellectual advances like accounting, timekeeping, refrigeration, communication, and transportation. Bernstein is a financial theorist who emphasizes great stories over dry factual detail.

Chaplin, Joyce E.
Round About the Earth: Circumnavigation from Magellan to Orbit. 2012. Simon and Schuster. 978-1416596196. 535pp.

Historian Chaplin looks at the experience of exploration and travel and the men and women who risked all to do what once seemed impossible—to physically circle our planet. Chaplin offers a "Geodrama" in three acts, each representing the mood of the circumnavigators of different eras. From Magellan to Captain Cook, the dominant mood was "fear," and more people actually perished than survived their trips; from the 1780s to the 1920s, the era of Darwin, Jules Verne, and Nellie Bly, the attitude was "confidence"; and in our own modern era of aviation and space travel, confidence has given way to "doubt"—as we begin to question our human dominance of the planet. This is a unique and engrossing armchair travel book that takes the reader from sail to steam to orbit, through time and across the globe.

Ekirch, A. Roger.
▶ *At Day's Close: Night in Times Past.* 2005. Norton. 0393050890. 447pp.

A richly detailed exploration of nighttime and all the magic, mystery, and mayhem it has contained. In former times, before private houses and public streets were illuminated, night meant the long stretch of darkness where the familiar world became unfamiliar and dangers abounded, but Ekirch gives equal time to night's pleasant contents as well—romance, reading, prayer, and sleep. Ekirch, a professor of history, explores novels, diaries, poetry, medical texts, municipal records, and a multitude of other primary sources to find evidence of men and women's experience of night in times past. The book contains an encyclopedic level of detail offering an intriguing exploration of an unexpected topic.

Ferguson, Niall.
The Ascent of Money: A Financial History of the World. **2008. Penguin.** 978-1594201929. 432pp.

Money, economics, and finance, historian Ferguson argues, are major cornerstones of civilization. Ferguson tells the history of the world through the prism of finance, looking at how our financial reality has evolved from simple trading to a system so complex that most modern people remain ignorant of its many sides—credit, markets, insurance, finance, and real estate.

Kotkin, Joel.
The City: A Global History. 2005. Modern Library. 978-0679603368. 218pp.

Kotkin explores the universality of the urban experience—why are humans drawn to cities, why do cities rise, and why do they decline? Urban culture flourishes, Kotkin argues, when three things are present: sacred places, security, and an atmosphere that promotes commerce and creativity. Nice chronology, excellent notes, and an essay listing "Suggested Reading" make this a valuable overview of one of humanity's enduring topics—where to live and why.

McWhorter, John.
The Power of Babel: A Natural History of Language. 2002. W. H. Freeman. 978-0716744733. 336pp.

Is human language 150,000 years old or merely 35,000 years old? Why are humans the only species on earth with complex language? Was there ever a time when all humanity spoke the same language? McWhorter, a professor at Berkeley, uses popular references and good humor to address these questions in this amiable introduction to the complex and arcane field of historical linguistics—the study of how language grows and changes across time and cultures. Follow up with *Empires of the Word: A Language History of the World* (2005) by Nicholas Ostler and *The Unfolding of Language: An Evolutionary Tour of Mankind's Greatest Invention* (2005) by Gary Deutscher.

Appendix: Authors to Explore

If reading history becomes a passion, continue your exploration with works by
these authors:

Ackroyd, Peter
Ambrose, Stephen
Beard, Mary
Brands, W. H.
Bryson, Bill
Cahill, Thomas
Cantor, Norman
Caro, Robert
Chernow, Ron
D'Este, Carlo
Dash, Mike
Davies, Norman
Dolin, Eric Jay
Ellis, Joseph
Everitt, Anthony
Fagan, Brian
Fernandez-Armesto, Felipe
Fischer, David Hackett
Foote, Shelby
Fraser, Antonia
Gelardi, Julia
Gill, Gillian
Goodwin, Doris Kearns

Hastings, Max
Hibbert, Christopher
Holland, Tom
Isaacson, Walter
Johnson, Paul
Johnson, Steven
Kagan, Donald
Keegan, John
Kurlansky, Mark
Larson, Erik
Lovell, Mary S.
Manchester, William
Massie, Robert K.
McCullough, David
Philbrick, Nathaniel
Schama, Simon
Sides, Hampton
Standage, Tom
Tuchman, Barbara
Ulrich, Laurel Thatcher
Weir, Alison
Winchester, Simon

Index

Bold entries are recommended but not annotated. * indicates fiction titles.

153

About the Author

TINA FROLUND is a librarian with the Las Vegas–Clark County Library District in Las Vegas, Nevada. She is the author of *Genrefied Classics: A Guide to Reading Interests in Classic Literature* (Libraries Unlimited, 2007) and the editor of *The Official YALSA Awards Guidebook* (2008).